Divorcing in Love

A HEART WARRIOR'S GUIDE TO
ENDING YOUR RELATIONSHIP
WITH INTENTIONAL ACTIONS
BASED IN LOVE

by Rebecca Harvey, Psy.D.

Divorcing in Love: A Heart Warrior's Guide to Ending Your Relationship with Intentional Actions Based in Love.

Heart Warriors Publication
6060 North Central Expressway,
Suite 616, Dallas, TX 75206

ISBN 978-1-09830-380-8

Heart
War

This book is dedicated to anyone struggling through the painful heartbreak of divorce and seeking a better way. I thank my dearest friends and family for your unwavering support during my own divorce. To the friends who uplifted me and offered their time and input toward the writing of this book—Julie, Jessica, Missy, Rebecca, and Stephanie—my deepest gratitude for your gifts.

A special thank you to my ex-husband, Randy—our marriage was brief, but our lessons in love ran deep. I am grateful for you.

Table of Contents

Book Cover Explanation

The cover art for this book is meant to represent "Kintsugi," a Japanese art form used to repair broken ceramics with a lacquer of powdered gold. The artistic repair celebrates scars as something not meant to be hidden, but owned as part of its history. Kintsugi translates to "golden repair," and it enhances and strengthens the once broken item, making it a completely new piece. This Japanese art teaches us that broken objects are not something to hide, but to proudly display, as more valuable than in original form. It takes considerable time for this artistic transformation process—but in the end, the item is more unique and resilient. I hope you embrace this metaphor as I did, to allow you to move through the painful or traumatic moments of divorce with hope... trusting you will come out more precious on the other end.

Preface

Despite urban legends that 50% of marriages will result in divorce, the rate of divorce actually peaked closer to 40% in 1980 and was predicted to rise. However, divorces have slowly declined since 1980, reaching an all-time low in 2016. Research indicates that a greater number of second marriages (close to 75%) will also end in divorce. Yet, those second marriages that do last will *report a substantially higher rate of marital satisfaction* than the roughly 60% of successful first-time marriages. This is an effect of wisdom: learning from our mistakes as well as gaining deeper insight into ourselves—our strengths, non-negotiable needs, and areas for personal growth, such as communication. The point? We are meant to learn the relationship lessons we need, whether with our current partner or a future partner.

As a therapist, I often encourage clients to consider the fact that even if they leave one situation, they are likely to encounter the same personal struggles in their next relationship. In many ways, they will simply pick up where they left off in their learning process—it just depends when they are ready to do the work.

We tend to select our partners and interact with them in patterned ways based on relationships from our childhood. Our own early relationship experiences with our caregivers, typically our parents, and the relationships we witness between those caregivers, shape the beliefs we develop about who we are and how the world operates. This includes our concept of what we believe a relationship looks like and how we should function within one. Unless we learn to practice otherwise, we move into our adult life carrying these same beliefs. As the saying goes, "Wherever you go, you take yourself with you." In other words, it is impossible for us to escape ourselves simply by ending a relationship. We cannot run away from our problems; and believe it or not, we create most of our problems. The only way to change the dynamics of a relationship is to change within ourselves. So, while you may find some different characteristics in a future partner, your basic issues will most likely remain the same.

With this knowledge, some individuals may be inspired to stay in their marriage and work through the difficulties of the present, particularly developing insight into opportunities for personal growth. We are all capable of changing once we identify what is not working for us, and, presumably, those are the same issues we are will be addressing at some point down the road, if we aspire to maintain a healthy relationship.

However, it can also be the case that we have learned what we needed to learn from a relationship, and it is time to let go and move forward in our journey. *I do not believe every marriage is meant to last a lifetime.* Life involves change. In fact, everything changes. Sometimes, this change includes ending relationships that we have outgrown...even if that is our marriage. Often, we wait too long to address the reality that it may be time to let go, and, instead, we begin to engage in unkind and unhealthy behaviors. There are many reasons we make the choice to stay. For some, it is based on a fear of being alone, for others, a belief that relationships must be "hard work" or that there is not an option to end a "bad marriage." We remain in marriage out of financial fear, religious beliefs, codependent needs, fear of hurting someone we love or upsetting other family members, or for concern of the impact on our children. Still others of us are merely repeating what was modeled by our parents, and we do not realize there is an alternate way to behave in a marriage. More reasons than these exist to justify staying in a marriage after it has otherwise reached its end. But the result of denying ourselves the option to let go almost always tends to cause pain for one, and usually both, partners.

A commonly asked question is, "How do I know if my marriage is over?" While it is a very personal decision, and one I believe you can only know by listening to your own inner voice, there are some signs that suggest your marriage journey may have reached its end. The greater number of negative signs you are experiencing, the more likely your marriage is in trouble or coming to an end. For instance, you may find yourself living the life of a single person—attending single-type functions or seeking considerable time away from your partner, not having sex with your partner, not communicating your personal and internal experiences, envisioning a future without them, considering or already having other sexual or romantic relationships, not feeling upset by the idea of your partner having another sexual or romantic relationship, no longer respecting your partner, or speaking to them with contempt or criticism. These signs, as well as many others not mentioned, suggest marital distress. If you refuse to attend therapy, or therapy isn't working, you may have come to the conclusion of your relationship.

In some relationships, the damage experienced from a partner's behavior is severe and longstanding. You may experience it as too pervasive to overcome, and, even if you were able to forgive, you might remain untrusting or unable to see your partner clearly...with love.

While this book will challenge you to consider whether divorce is the only option available to achieve a more peaceful life, it is not intended as a roadmap to help you decide *if* you should divorce your partner. Rather, this book is aimed at helping you be attentive and purposeful with your decision-making process around divorce. It serves as a guide to your internal mindset during your divorce process as you find a loving way to move forward. I suggest slowing down your process and finding a pace best suited to your ultimate goal of treating yourself and your partner with respect so that you may feel as positive as possible about your decision, whether you choose to stay or go. Slowing down will offer the opportunity for your *presence*, or conscious awareness of your thoughts, feelings, and behaviors, throughout the entire process, from decision about divorce to conclusion and beyond.

This book also touches on a few legal considerations, with the intention to spark creative approaches. Entering legal counsel with an open mind may help you settle on the best arrangement. In no way is this book attempting to offer legal advice. While I will add considerations of the technical process of divorce from the framework of a "loving divorce," I am not a legal professional. The laws and legal processes differ across locations, and the ideas suggested in this book may not be feasible in some places. For all legal counsel, each person must seek guidance in their own state and consult a licensed attorney.

This book also offers considerations for those of you with children. While I am not a child therapist, I believe in honoring your child's experience of this process as well, as this is crucial to their well-being.

Throughout this book, I will use the terms "partner," "ex," "spouse," or "estranged spouse/partner" interchangeably to reflect the differing places that readers may be in their contemplation of, or action in the divorce process. It is my hope that readers will move through these terms with ease, rather than finding themselves hung up on a term that does not seem to fit their personal framework or marital situation. Furthermore, although this book will use the term "marriage," for simplicity of concept, romantic commitment can take many forms. It is my intention and belief that anyone ending a long-term romantic relationship can find effective support in these pages.

Despite your best intentions to end your relationship from a place of love, at moments, you may find the concepts in the book difficult or seemingly impossible. Much like other difficult life experiences, it can be beneficial to take space from time to time. Allow yourself permission to come back to reading this book in those moments when you have centered back into your commitment to end your relationship with love.

Introduction

"Divorce." What an emotionally provocative word. As common as divorce is in our society, it still remains a fairly taboo topic. We fear this word, even prior to saying "I do" and some use that fear as a rationale to never marry. Those in a relationship may threaten this word to persuade their partner to make changes. At some point, often after a long and exhausting battle with our once beloved mate, we might come to embrace this word and the hope of peace it can bring.

For both married and un-married, the "D word" frightens us. It is perceived as the ultimate relationship failure. In fact, research suggests many people wait until later in life to marry in hopes of avoiding the pain and perceived embarrassment of divorce. The average age of entering into a first marriage has increased, and, interestingly enough, so has the number of marriages in the United States. Yet, it would be nearly impossible to find an adult who has not witnessed the proverbial "fight to the death" between two people who once celebrated the depth of their love and commitment.

What if you could end your relationship as you started it…with kindness, respect, compassion, and love? Right now, that idea may seem impossible—you may be certain I am out of my mind for even suggesting it. But *I truly believe every life experience is an opportunity for growth, healing, and broadening our capacity for love.*

If you are reading this, chances are you are either in the divorce process or contemplating divorce. As a therapist, I have helped many people through their decisions regarding separation and divorce. I have worked with them during and in the aftermath of divorce. It can be a scary, confusing, and isolating process. Many of you reading this book are in some amount of distress and likely seeking relief from the discomfort of your marriage. Divorce may or may not be the best path for your relationship at this time. However, if you decide divorce is right for you, it is my hope to help you find as much peace and support as possible during your divorce process.

Consideration of divorce often comes on the heels of one or both spouses feeling betrayed, disappointed, humiliated, or otherwise let down. Other times, a couple has muscled through the discomfort of negative interactions, yet allowed the emotional connection between them to suffer a slow death until there is no longer interest or emotional investment in the relationship. Couples may refer to this slow disengagement process as "growing apart." Typically, in these situations, both parties have placed their energies into other areas instead of investing in one another. In this way, relationships, including marriages, can be seen as having a "reason, season, or lifetime." Again, not all relationships are meant to last "'til death do us part." *Sometimes, it is only in marriage that we learn the lessons needed for our emotional and spiritual evolution. We are here on earth for that evolution—to learn to be more loving in the world—and this "love" is not just about how we treat others, but how we treat ourselves, including learning self-care and healthy boundaries.* Relationships in general serve as a mirror, highlighting areas we need to explore for our personal growth. Sometimes a relationship, even our marriage, is intended to help us learn necessary lessons so we can proceed forward in life with greater awareness, wisdom, and maturity.

Still, the word *divorce* seems to set people on edge. Even those who have never been married or are contently married offer advice to their divorcing friends. They offer such counsel as: "Make sure you are the first one to lawyer up!"; "Take him for all he's got!"; or "You better protect yourself and start hiding assets." Further panic can be brought on by seeking professional legal counsel, as even an attorney with the best intentions can incite fear and a stance of justified attack or defensive retaliation into the mind of those considering divorce. I was once told by a divorce attorney, "Most attorneys really do believe they're doing their client a service by protecting their interests. But attorneys are people who were drawn to the field because they are good at fighting and winning!" Attorneys are walking alongside their clients, strategizing amidst the all-too-common experiences of fear, anger, grief, and desire for retaliation—the steps that make up the typical divorce. As a result, they FIGHT. TO. WIN.

However, there is always another way. It is possible to move through your divorce in a manner that reduces pain and leaves each of you with a greater sense of peace. It's easy to be loving when things are going well, when we actively like the people with whom we are engaging. But stretching our capacity to love broadly, as we evolve in our journey through life, takes work. It is the courageous work of a warrior—to face our fears and mistakes and move in the direction of acceptance and forgiveness.

When we accept the challenge to take a loving stance in all situations, we are operating as a *Heart Warrior*. Heart Warriors demonstrate love in trying times with difficult people, not just the people we enjoy when they are behaving as we would like. It isn't always easy to remember, but your partner is a human being, struggling with their own pain and fear. This awareness sometimes alludes us, because pain and fear are often expressed with defensiveness, attacks, aggression, withdrawal, or avoidance. If we choose to remember we are all human and we all fall short of perfection, we can transcend the transgressions we experience and evolve mentally, emotionally, and spiritually in the midst of our struggles.

As I began writing this book, I had just filed for divorce. It had only been four days since the paperwork was filed. We agreed to a controlled separation (in-home) in April, moved to separate homes in June, decided via couples therapy to divorce in November, and, in February, the paperwork was filed. Despite my strong sense early on that this was the best option for me, I requested we pace the divorce as a slow and conscious process—luckily, my partner was willing.

My friends questioned why it was dragging on. My answer, "I'm f**king exhausted!" The truth is, I *was* tired. I was also frightened, ashamed, and worn out from feeling all the negative emotions my marriage ignited in me. I wanted to reconnect with the better parts of myself—and as quickly as possible! Toward the end of my marriage, it was as if my spiritual and self-care behaviors were no longer yielding the results they had previously. *I needed to get back in touch with the version of me I liked.* I also had an idealistic hope that if I could regulate my emotions and be present with each step of the process, I could avoid a knock-down, drag-out fight to the death, and instead, create a peaceful and kind ending of my relationship. The philosophies I upheld in my work as a psychologist suggested it could be done; so, I decided to give it my best effort.

Based on this decision, you may imagine me to be a passive or "soft" individual. Let me clear that misperception up right now! I have been described by others as "Type-A personality." I am dynamic and outspoken—I do not shy away from confrontation. While I am not someone who "rages out" on others, I *am* quick to my experience of frustration and at times, comfortable with expressing it...with what might be described as unfortunate ease. One of my biggest flaws is my reactive tendency to lapse into critical judgment, which, when paired with the emotional perspicacity and verbal fluency of a psychologist, can be an unpleasant position for the person on the other end. So, to be quite clear, I am *highly capable* of perpetuating a knockdown, drag-out fight. But to be transparent, by the time I reached my decision to divorce, I was very clear I was DONE FIGHTING with this man! What I wanted was to take back my emotions, reclaim my body (as emotional stress had begun to create unexplained somatic illness, body pain, and stomach ulcers), and recover my inner peace and sense of joy. The only way I could see to accomplish this was to "divorce in love."

Reading these two words in the same sentence may seem outrageous to you. Believe me, I heard the disbelief and the skepticism from those around me. But those who *truly knew* me, understood that this was totally possible for me. And, if it was possible for me, it is possible for even the strongest of personalities. What is unique about me is that I love *deeply* and strive to see the best in others. I operate on the belief that even when I am disappointed, hurt, or angry, others are doing the best they can in each moment, just as I am. From this place of compassion, I *can forgive*— even when no one is seeking forgiveness. Forgiveness does not require closure or any effort or apology from another. It is a choice, and, what's more, a choice made *by you* and *for you.*

I am writing this book for the Heart Warriors of the world, those people who believe there must be a better way to simultaneously honor and let go of the relationship they once valued above all others. What I am offering is an alternative option to the overly common perception of divorce. *You can create a loving and kind divorce process in which you honor your journey together as you navigate your journey apart.* Even if your partner is not willing to embark on this journey from a mutual perspective of love, you can apply these principles to greatly impact your own experience and reduce suffering. I do not however suggest this will be a pleasant experience. Pain is pain; and the grief associated with the loss will cause pain. But, when we reduce our contribution of drama, we greatly reduce the *suffering from* our experience.

While you may find after reading this book that you wish to reconsider your decision for divorce, you will also find ways to create purposeful space in your divorce process, if you elect to move forward on that path. Creating mental and emotional space can help you gain a better perspective on your marital dynamics, your personal needs, and your options for honoring your marriage in the midst of divorce. For those of you who elect to move forward with divorce, I hope this book will inspire ways to facilitate a more peaceful divorce process, allowing you to honor yourself, your spouse, and your marriage as best you can.

You will also find practical solutions, such as advice in selecting your attorney or mediator, understanding your options for divorce process, ways to pace your divorce to suit your own needs, and how to engage in important discussions while managing strong emotions. Additionally, to support your growth and learning process, there will be exercises to increase personal insight, develop compassion, find forgiveness, as well as exercises for supporting yourself through your grief process. *Lastly, and something I believe is unique to this book, you will find solo and partnered ceremonies for honoring and letting go of your marriage and meditation exercises for releasing your marital relationship in a healthy manner.* Please strongly consider using these exercises to facilitate the emotional processing involved in ending your relationship. You may find it helpful to keep a notebook on hand for completing the questions and exercises offered in the book.

It is my hope that using this book will help you gain clarity along your divorce journey. Additionally, I hope it will prepare you for your post-divorce new life, offering ways to learn from your past relationship and prepare you for your most ideal future.

Section I

INITIAL PREPARATION FOR DIVORCING IN LOVE

"There are two basic motivating forces: fear and love. When we are afraid, we pull back from life. When we are in love, we open to all that life has to offer with passion, excitement, and acceptance. We need to learn to love ourselves first, in all our glory and our imperfections. If we cannot love ourselves, we cannot fully open to our ability to love others or our potential to create. Evolution and all hopes for a better world rest in the fearlessness and open-hearted vision of people who embrace life."

– John Lennon

Rebecca Harvey, Psy. D.

Chapter 1

Preparing Your Post-Divorce Vision

*"Vision without action is merely a dream...
Vision with action can change the world."*

– Joel A. Barker

To begin, I'll strongly encourage you to pause here in order to create a vision for the outcome of your divorce. While not everyone reading this book will decide to divorce, it is important, if you're considering divorce, to envision your life afterward. Decide first how you want to *feel* at the conclusion. Then imagine the scenario that supports this desired feeling. The vision of this future scenario will be your guidepost throughout your divorce process. Every step of your divorce process will be influenced by the experience you want to have at the conclusion of your divorce—from the manner in which you speak, to the choices you make dividing assets or establishing custody arrangements. This is an important first step, as without a post-divorce vision, you might easily lose sight of the bigger picture and be swept away by your emotional impulses.

On the following page, you will find an exercise to assist you in creating your post-divorce vision. As you create your vision, try to remove limitations of what you think you or your partner is capable of doing. In other words, if you

3

suddenly had a "magic wand," how would you design your future relationship with your ex and others in your life? You are not working under the constraints of how you see things today, you are working on a vision of what the future could be—and how you will contribute to that end goal. The idea here is a concept of shooting for the moon, and, if you miss, you will land among the stars. Dig deep and aim high with your future goal. Making this effort will serve you far better than failing to make a plan for a positive outcome. When we leave things to chance in these kinds of situations, emotions (likely negative) tend to lead—and that doesn't fare well for anyone involved. My personal and professional experiences have shown me that individuals can divorce kindly and retain positive feelings for one another both during and after their divorce.

Creating Your Post-Divorce Vision

As you consider your vision, keep in mind you are working on an *ideal vision,* not what you imagine is possible at this moment. It is certainly helpful to keep it realistic in the general sense of the word, but you do not need to account for what you imagine your partner or other people in your life are currently capable of mentally or emotionally. If you find yourself letting this limit your vision, consciously allow some space for the idea that you might be pleasantly surprised with your own future behavior and the behavior of your ex.

To begin, allow yourself to run down the list provided below to determine how you would like to feel with and about each person following your divorce. For instance, you may want to have a pleasant relationship with your in-laws. While you cannot fully control their behavior, you can definitely do your part to keep things amicable and kind. Take a full minute or more with each person on this list below and imagine what your relationship could look like in the future. Think about what that might require from you now as you move through your divorce process.

Take your time with this exercise, as it is the main factor in determining your desired divorce outcome. First, allow yourself to "try on" each of these relationships as you envision how you'd like to experience them in the future. Second, write down three to five ideas that describe *how you'd like to feel*. Third, give yourself three to five guidelines about *how you will need to behave* to achieve this.

As an example, while some mutual friends will pick "sides," in my situation, it was important to me that no one felt that they must do so and could instead retain relationships with both of us. This meant that I could not use those individuals for my emotional support. Otherwise, when I struggled, I might have inadvertently "pulled" them to my "side."

Example: Mutual Friends

Desired Feelings:
1. Open and relaxed
2. Included and connected
3. Respected

Necessary Behavior:
1. Speak respectfully about my ex
2. Not vent frustrations
3. Remain in contact with these friends

Relationships to Consider:

- **Yourself**—How do you want to feel about yourself? This will be the direct result of how you behave during this time.

- **Your Ex**—Do you want to be able to be friendly or feel at peace when you run into one another in public?

- **Your Children**—How do you want them to perceive you and your ex? What do you want them to learn? How do you want your children to treat you and your ex? The way you respond to your ex will impact their perspectives and thus impact how they treat you in the future.

- **Your Family**—How do you want them to support you now and later? Think consciously on this. Not all of us are able to seek support from our family without judgement, manipulation, or attempts by them to intrude or control. Take some time to consider what is realistic and how you want things to look at completion.

- **Your In-Laws**—Whether or not you maintain a relationship with them, consider how do *you* want to feel about them and for them to feel about you?

- **Mutual Friends**—Take a moment from a calm and non-vengeful place to decide, how do you want your mutual friends to feel about you and your ex, post-divorce?

- **Social Acquaintances**—Mutual people you may encounter at various shared events may not be a high priority for you, but what kind of emotional energy would you prefer to feel in their presence?

- **Mutual Service People**—You may share the same service people following your divorce, like dog walkers or babysitters. For example, I still share a housekeeper with my ex, and it was important to me that she not feel uncomfortable. I did not want her to hear me speak about my ex with anything but kind words, nor put her in the awkward position of discussing my ex and his new life. What can you do to support (or if desired, release) your relationship with any mutual service people?

- **Co-Workers**—Consider briefly, how much information will help you be supported in your workplace and how much information invites unwanted attention and input even after your divorce?

Additional Considerations

- Would you like to have a feeling of peace and contentment, as opposed to anguish and contempt?

- Do you want to eventually feel more kindness toward your partner?

- How do you want to feel emotionally when you run into your partner in public or social settings?

- Would you like to be friendly with them?

- Would you like to feel happy when you see them move on in a positive way with their life?

- Would you like to call upon your ex when you need a special skill or insight they can provide?

- How do you want your children to feel?

- What do you want your children to learn about managing disagreements?

- How would you like your children to treat those with whom they disagree?

- What do you want the quality and tone of your life and children's life to be in general?

- Would you like to spend holidays together as a "modern family"?

**Use this space to brainstorm on your
Post-Divorce Vision:**

_____

_____

_____

_____

_____

I encourage you to revisit this vision often throughout your divorce process, not just when reading this book. One thing that might be helpful is to imagine specific future events and how you would like to feel during those events. This can be an upcoming child's birthday party or your ten-year-old's wedding in fifteen to twenty years. Understandably, this might be challenging to do when you are feeling particularly upset with your partner. If needed, revisit this exercise at a time when you are feeling more in touch with your "highest self," or more loving nature. Using meditation or visualization, like the exercises throughout the book and in Section V, may be one way to get in touch with your truest loving nature. Allow yourself to re-envision this goal from that healthier mental space.

Several months after finalizing my divorce, my ex and I were asked to walk, arm-in-arm, down the aisle as part of the bridal party for a wedding of two close friends. Had we ended things in a hostile manner, this would have been uncomfortable for everyone and potentially caused an unfortunate strain on an otherwise beautiful celebration. Because we were friendly, we were able to fully enjoy the destination wedding, appreciate one another's company at the reception, and laugh at the irony of the predicament in which we found ourselves.

Some years later, when the building in which I leased therapy space informed me that they would be forcing me out of my beloved office, I was able to call on my ex to assist me with negotiations of the transaction—something in which he is very skilled. I was thankful to have his expertise, and (I think) he was happy to be of assistance. Despite our decision not to share our lives together, we are able to appreciate and call upon one another when needed. The dynamic feels relaxed and pleasant, and we have both expressed gratitude for what we learned from one another and for being able to retain a unique post-divorce relationship.

Despite intensely negative experiences in my marriage, I was still able to keep in mind my desire to feel good about myself throughout my divorce. In each instance where I upheld my decision to be kind and respectful, my ex ultimately responded by meeting me in that place of kindness. It wasn't easy, and we both had our moments, but the tone we set, and the slower pace we allowed, helped us stay focused on our goal...Divorcing in Love.

Chapter 1 Tools:

• Consider your post-divorce vision, using the questions provided, prior to moving forward. What do you hope your life will look like when the divorce dust has settled? Truly think about how you want to feel. Focus intently on that positive experience—so much that you may even feel it in your body.

• Take another moment to consider what doubts and fears you have about the process of divorcing in love. What emotional obstacles will you need to be aware of, so that they do not unconsciously interrupt your efforts? You may want to write these down in the space below so you can keep an eye out for them and be prepared to work through these specific issues as you move through the book and through your divorce process.

_____

_____

_____

_____

Chapter 2

Managing Your Mindset: The Importance of Shifting Your Perspective

"It's not what happens to you, but how you react to it that matters."

– Epictetus

It may be difficult to conceive that your spouse, who you may resent right now, was once one of the most special people in your world. I certainly wouldn't suggest that the pain or betrayal they may have caused you is deserved, justified, or okay. But we are all human. If we are truly honest with ourselves, we can all be selfish, jealous, deceptive, angry, needy, controlling, critical, withholding, and plain old mean to differing degrees at different moments in our life. A short-sighted comment I often hear clients say in regard to being hurt by their partner is "I would never do something like that to someone." I believe my clients are being honest when they say this. However, the truth is, we very rarely know what we are capable of until we are pushed past our threshold and find ourselves behaving in ways "unlike" ourselves. Once we admit that we are all capable of hurting others, we can begin the process of extending compassion to all. Compassion is important because it is the first step on the path to forgiveness, and this forgiveness will set you free emotionally.

Right now, it may sound impossible, and you may feel an adverse reaction at your very core when considering extending compassion or forgiveness to your partner. You may want to say to me, "You wouldn't agree if you knew what my partner did (or how they treated me)." Believe me, I can relate to this perspective. But, if you are able to quiet your mind and listen to your inner voice, the voice that comes from a place of love, you will likely, in time, be able to access your desire for forgiveness. *Letting go of your pain about your relationship is essential to move forward in a healthy way.* Trust that, as you move forward in an intentional manner, you will find ways to release your pain.

Many people scoff at the idea of *Divorcing in Love* as they assert how much they truly *hate* their once-adored partner. I have heard my clients express that it would be impossible to find any loving feelings amidst the depths of hate they currently feel. So, let's take a look at the word "hate."

One of my favorite philosophers, Rollo May, stated, "Hate is not the opposite of love; apathy is." This sentence holds so much truth. *HATE IS NOT THE OPPOSITE OF LOVE,* despite the commonly held misconception. Hate is better understood as "love disappointed" or "love unrequited." The true opposite of love is apathy or indifference. When we love someone, and they do not value, treat, or love us in

14

the way we believe we deserve, we are, at the very least, disappointed. When we express that disappointment and are still unable to obtain the treatment we seek from our partner, we may find ourselves slipping into feelings of contempt, resentment, and even "hate."

If we can begin to accept that the feelings of hate actually stem from an original place of love, we may be more inclined to move toward a loving divorce process. After all, most people are not moving through divorce in a state of *apathy*—a lack of emotion one way or the other for their partner. Those who disagree might reflect on whether their "sense" of apathy is actually emotional detachment from feelings about your partner. One way to test this is to consider some recent experiences that have led you to contemplate divorce. Certainly, these memories stir some emotional response in you. The emotion you experience, as you think of these memories, verifies that you are not in a state of apathy regarding your partner. Next, if you are able to let yourself move into deeper awareness, beyond the initial feeling of anger or hate to the place where this heavy emotion originated, you are likely to find hurt and disappointment. It is reasonable to feel hurt and disappointed. You made yourself vulnerable by opening your heart to your partner, and now, you feel let down.

When I have shared the idea that apathy is truly the opposite of love with my clients and they respond by asserting their feelings of apathy, it doesn't take much exploration to reveal that they have many emotions, however blocked off they may prefer to feel from those emotions in the moment. In fact, often the outward stance of indifference (i.e., "I don't care if she dies") is a defense against awareness of deeper conflicting feelings of love, alongside hurt and anger.

Moving from our deepest loving commitment to a genuine place of having no feelings whatsoever toward our partner is very unlikely. However, having feelings of hurt, anger, shame, sadness, remorse, guilt, and so on, is very common and often the fuel behind a nasty divorce process. Awareness of this deeper emotional experience is the place where your healing will need to originate. *No amount of unfavorable emotion is reason enough to justify a battle that ultimately robs you of your peace and happiness.*

Exercise Invitation: Shift Your Thinking

Stop trying to solve the problem of your emotions or decide the ways you would like your partner to change, particularly if you have decided to let go of the relationship. Instead, focus on accepting what is, rather than continuing to lament what you wish had been. There is tremendous suffering to bear when we choose to "wallow" in our disappointment.

It is important to have enough compassion for ourselves that we stop fixating on things we cannot control and shift our focus elsewhere entirely. Practicing mindfulness can assist with conditioning your brain to redirect your thoughts to ones that will serve you better in the moment. Meditation can also be an effective "distraction" from your pain. Keep in mind that attempting to meditate in a particularly heightened state of emotional arousal is not an effective strategy. You must practice this instead during moments that are free from intense distress. This is how a meditation practice is helpful—you build the skill that you can then more easily call upon during difficult moments.

The key to effective application of cognitive redirection is making a choice to move your thoughts to something else, rather than wasting time and emotions spinning in upsetting, unproductive thought patterns.

For your practice, bring to mind a time when you felt completely relaxed and happy.

Recall where you were, what you were doing, and what was going on around you. Notice how you feel in your body to really enrich the experience. Now bring a thought to mind of something that recently was irritating or upsetting with your ex or about your divorce. It might help to start with something relatively small to illustrate this exercise, like a level 2-3 rating on a scale of 10, with 10 being most disturbing. You can always practice with bigger things once you feel more comfortable with the practice. Now notice yourself thinking about the upsetting thought and make the choice to stop and switch over to the positive experience you just had in your mind. Stay with that positive experience until you feel your emotions and body sensations begin to shift back into a positive state.

If you'd like, you can move back and forth between the two thoughts, noting how your emotional experience changes. You may notice that it is easier to get "sucked in" by your negative thoughts. This is natural but can interrupt your effort to stay in a positive emotional space.

> *Notice that you can switch gears to the positive thought by exerting a willful effort. Recognizing you have this ability reminds you that you do not have to stay spinning in your negative thought patterns but can redirect to different thoughts whenever it is beneficial for you.*

One way of discovering the deeper feelings you may have about your partner is to look at your unmet expectations and your lost hopes. It may help to understand that you are grieving your loss of some of your biggest dreams—whether you realize it or not. Grieving during divorce is not a simple one-step process. You may grieve many aspects of your marriage, *even if it was not the best fit in all areas.* You may find you grieve in distinctly separate moments as you let go of a friend, a travel companion, a sexual partner, a financial provider, or a co-parent. Considering all the hopes and dreams you are releasing when you release your partner, don't be surprised if your grief seems to "sneak up on you" at unexpected moments. The good news is, if you elect to divorce, you are exchanging these expired hopes for new dreams for your life.

Some people assert, "I never loved my partner to begin with, so I'm not grieving them." It's true, some people marry for circumstance, like pregnancy, family arrangement, or social expectations. In these cases, I ask you to acknowledge that you at least agreed, with some level of hope, to build a life with someone. You likely had warm feelings about how things would play out for you. While those feelings may now be absent, it is my hope that you are reading this with a personal desire to cultivate a sense of peace for yourself. Ending things with your partner on good terms is a good way to begin.

My point is, regardless of the situation, divorce feels disappointing on some level. If we can begin to accept our feelings of disappointment, we become more resilient. While it may prove challenging, even with the best intentions, we can cultivate our loving presence as we simultaneously end our relationship. It is important to understand that it is possible

> It is important to understand that it is possible to find peace in the midst of inherent disappointment and dissatisfaction.

find peace in the midst of inherent disappointment. To accomplish this, we must be mindful of our thoughts, feelings, and actions. It is only from this position of self-awareness that we can call upon the necessary qualities of *compassion, acceptance, respect, vulnerability,* and *courage.* This book is intended to help you bring about these qualities—and, to be very clear, they are within all of us. The mere fact that you are willing to read this book shows that you are capable of approaching your relationship's end as a **Heart Warrior**, by divorcing in love. One of the most important steps to creating a loving divorce is to center yourself in a space of compassion as often as possible. Do this both for yourself and for those around you. Discussion of this and techniques for cultivation of compassion will be offered in this book.

The reason compassion becomes so difficult at times is because it is quite easy in the midst of our pain to become focused only on our own perspective and place the blame squarely outside ourselves. You may think that the affair, the financial betrayal, the horrible words, the neglect, or the attempts to manipulate and control occurred in an isolated bubble, not impacted by your behavior. You may firmly assert the problems were their fault alone and were *the sole reason* the marriage suffered. I'm here to tell you **this is not the case.**

To be clear, none of the aforementioned behaviors are acceptable in a relationship, but, with a few exceptions (like sociopathic predator behavior), most of these transgressions were a response to an already dysfunctional marital dynamic. In other words, you also contributed, in some way, to your relationship dynamic, though you may not currently see it. For that matter, even the infamous sociopathic, narcissistic, or borderline personality disordered individual needs someone willing to play the rescuer, enabler, codependent, or victim role. We cannot truly pass all the blame to our partner, regardless of their transgressions.

Taking a personal inventory of your own contributions is an important way to start the healing process during and following divorce. Conducting this inventory in the beginning stages of divorce allows you to increase your capacity to give compassion and forgiveness both to yourself and your partner, in order to ease the emotional distress of the divorce process. This can reduce unnecessary emotional pain and jumpstart the very necessary grieving and healing journey ahead. But first, you must ensure you are emotionally and mentally prepared for the journey. Section II will focus on this preparation.

One-Sided Loving Divorce

What if, you may wonder, my partner is not willing to engage in a loving divorce process? Recently, while appearing on a podcast to discuss healthy divorce, I was challenged by one of the hosts with the assumption that some people would not be able to take on a loving divorce process, even if they wanted one. While I agree that not everyone will have a mutually supported vision for a loving divorce, it is still possible for *you* to have a loving divorce. What I mean by this is simple: your partner does not have to be on board with a loving divorce plan for you to engage in a loving divorce process and dramatically alter your own experience. Certainly, when both parties are even somewhat in agreement, it will ease the process and improve the total outcome. But do not underestimate your own personal actions. They will impact both your emotional experience and the experience your partner has, which may alter how they respond to you. Using this book to guide you in the process of divorcing in love can only improve your emotional experience both during and after your divorce. Reducing your toxic exchanges, managing your emotions, moving through your divorce with a mindful presence, holding on to your integrity, finding personal growth opportunities, and keeping some peace of mind is all possible if you commit to the process of divorcing in love.

As an example, consider what happens when you elect to remain angry with someone who has hurt you. You think of them and feel negative emotions and physical sensations. You may find yourself thinking of this often and imagining what you might have done differently or could say in the future if you encounter this person. Each time you think of this, you reside in a state of anger, as if it is currently happening. Meanwhile, the person you are angry with may be sipping a piña colada on a beach in the Bahamas, perfectly happy, smiling and enjoying the sunshine. In that moment, your anger only impacts you. Only you get to decide what you think about, what you do, and how you feel. *You get to decide if you have a loving divorce process...and if you're lucky, your partner will decide to have one as well.*

Chapter 2 Tools:

- Consider that we are all flawed humans. Perhaps, this will help you develop some basic compassion for your estranged partner. In the space below, answer the following questions: Are you placing all the blame for the disappointing parts of the marriage on your partner, or are you able to own some of your unhelpful contributions? What can you identify as their contributions to the marriage dissolving? What unhealthy contributions can you own as your own?

- Remember that your negative feelings are derived from your disappointment in not being loved or treated as you expected you would be when you entered into your marriage. Take a brief moment to see if you can get in touch with the simultaneous feelings of love and disappointment you may be experiencing? Can you entertain the idea that we can be happy while we simultaneously experience dissatisfaction with life's situations?

- Do you want to allow pain from the past to rob you of the peace and happiness you deserve? Can you commit to your own loving divorce regardless of your partner's participation? If the answer is no, take some time to journal what is holding you back from this choice, and revisit it as you move through the book.

_____

_____

_____

_____

_____

_____

_____

_____

_____

_____

Section II

EMOTIONAL PREPARATION FOR DIVORCING IN LOVE

As you consider or prepare for your divorce, it is important to stabilize yourself mentally, emotionally, and physically. Doing so will provide you the tools to perform clear decision making and keep the rest of your life functioning in a reasonable manner. Those who do not focus on self-support during this time might find stress piling up when parenting or working. This buildup of stress not only takes a toll on your health and well-being, it may actually contribute to poor choices and poor performance across all areas of life and relationships. In reality, it is possible to find balance and keep yourself in a healthy and relatively peaceful position throughout your divorce process. The most effective strategy for a healthy divorce begins with a willingness to shift your perspective. A technique that is useful for assisting with this is mindfulness, specifically the practice of mindful self-awareness.

Mindfulness creates the foundation for learning to see things more clearly. To be able to separate out your needs, emotions, and responses moment by moment. Mindfulness is the basis for healthy communication, boundary work, spiritual connection, and self-care. So, let us begin by exploring how your loving divorce will be foundationally based in the important practice of mindfulness.

27

Chapter 3

Minding Mindfulness

"Moment to moment, breath to breath
...be here now."

– Rebecca Harvey

Mindfulness is quite likely a term you've heard, as the concept has been receiving increased attention in the last few years due to its vast benefits. Science now confirms the healing benefits that contemplative practices and religions have been implementing for centuries. Mindfulness is simply defined as sustained awareness of our experience of thought, emotion, physical sensation, and our environment in each present moment. Breath to breath, current moment to next current moment, mindfulness is the constant renewing of our mind through attention to our experience of "the now." Mindful awareness can be cultivated through meditation or through the simple act of consciously being aware in each moment. For example, as you read these words, you may also have awareness of the feel of this book in your hands. You may see the letters on the page. You may be aware of the background noise around you, like a ticking clock or a barking dog. As you observe your experience in this present moment, a transformation begins to occur in the neural structure of your brain, allowing for an increased capacity of self-observation—you are increasing mindful awareness.

One approach to mindfulness and mindful meditation is to increase our general awareness of the present moment, noticing each time our focus is distracted. When we observe that we have become distracted, we give attention to the distraction by acknowledging it as having occurred and then return our attention to the present moment.

Therapeutic Invitation:

Pause here and notice your breath for the next seven to ten breaths. Notice whether it is easy or difficult to stay focused only on your breath...

As you reflect back on those several breaths, recall whether you became distracted. Was it easy to maintain focus only on your breath? If you did become distracted, what specifically grabbed your attention and thoughts? Remember that simply observing and being present with what you notice cultivates mindfulness and supports brain structures that help you regulate your emotions more effectively!

Having completed the exercise above, take note that distractions are not something to worry about. As soon as you notice you have become distracted, you are practicing mindfulness again, as you have just become aware of your present experience of "distraction." An important aspect of mindfulness practice is that we refrain from judging ourselves and instead accept ourselves where we are—focused or distracted. Instead of criticizing, we simply notice the interruption of our focus and immediately release it. An amazing thing occurs as we begin to practice this skill; we become more aware of the patterns of our mind, noticing our mental and emotional tendencies. As these patterns emerge, we see the multitude of thoughts and emotions moving through our mind during any given moment. We may experience some of these as favorable, some as uncomfortable.

When we can accept what we observe in ourselves without judgement, we can begin to see how similar we are to one another as humans. We have our more favored "shiny" parts that we love to show and talk about. We also have our "less shiny" parts—which we may want to hide or prefer not to notice, let alone broadcast publicly. We can practice extending our capacity for self-compassion over and over while we observe these patterns, by recognizing that we all have the less shiny parts and we all experience every emotion on the spectrum...even the "bad" ones! When we begin to accept this and practice our compassion, the natural byproduct is an increased ability to extend this compassion to others—including our partner (or estranged partner) and our children. Whether or not we choose to share what we observe, the mere act of noticing mindfully without judgment will still physically change our brain, and therefore, our experiences in life.

Chapter 3 Tools:

- Throughout your day or while you're going to sleep, take a few moments to notice your breath. Are you able to stay present with it for a brief time and to notice when your mind becomes distracted?

- Try a few times a day to say: "I am aware," or "I am present with this moment," and then notice what you sense around you.

- Once you have some practice using mindful breath awareness and notice your mind in a calmer state, can you more easily identify your shiney and less shiney parts? In other words, what qualities emerge as more favorable within you and which traits do you see as needing further development? Revisit this question at a time when you have been able to mindfully slow your thoughts. Attempt to observe without judgement.

REBECCA HARVEY, PSY. D.

Chapter 4

Cultivating Compassion

"True spirituality means entering the arena of life with a heart of compassion and then doing the best we can."

– David N. Elkins

Using mindful presence to cultivate compassion is the key to your emotional well-being during your divorce or consideration of divorce. *Compassion* is defined as a deep sympathy about the suffering of another, coupled with a desire to alleviate that suffering. In the practice of *self-compassion,* we extend our sympathy to ourselves. It really doesn't matter whether you begin to cultivate your skills of personal compassion by first learning to extend it to others (like your pet or child) and then extending it more regularly to yourself, or if you begin with yourself and then move on to others. The cool thing about this skill is that compassion begins to "generalize." Like a slow burn, compassion spreads to other situations over time.

Practicing compassion will allow you to create a mental space for yourself *and* your partner to reflect honestly on your marriage. It will also sustain you through the difficult ups and downs of your divorce process, should you elect to move in that direction. Divorce can wreak havoc on your sense of self-worth and damage parts of your self-image, which may already be fragile after the struggles within your marriage. Being trained in the art of self-compassion will help you offset the damage that divorce can bring.

Dr. Kristin Neff identifies self-compassion as a better predictor of happiness, mood stability, and positive self-regard than self-esteem. In fact, self-compassion holds all of the benefits of self-esteem, without the downside, which is this: When we are beholden to our sense of self-esteem, we see it plummet when we perceive ourselves as "losing." And, since divorce is often experienced as a failure, it is imperative that we avoid trying to rebuild ourselves with a focus only on our self-esteem.

When we find ourselves in relational disputes, a focus on building or salvaging our ego often translates to a stance of needing to win or be the one in the "right"—making the other person "wrong." This "right vs. wrong" mentality may lead to unproductive behavior and can leave one or both partners feeling disempowered, victimized, or misunderstood. When compassion is the focus instead of blame, we can work toward acceptance of differences in the other. A focus on self-compassion helps us become more accepting of all of our personality traits and behaviors, including those parts of ourselves that we may not like very much. In time, we can do the same for our partner—*even with the parts of them we currently cannot tolerate.*

Cultivating compassion is an important aspect of mental and emotional health. Regardless of whether you decide to remain in your marriage or not, developing your capacity for compassion will serve you well. In fact, mental health researchers have found those who rank high in compassion report less emotional upset when working through relational conflict. It was suggested that they are better able to calm themselves and thus respond to conflict with a more peaceful approach, "in a way that balances the needs of the self and others."[1] It was suggested that those who struggle to feel compassion either *over-* or *under-*prioritize their needs in relation to their partner's needs. Those who have developed self-compassion can keep both their needs and the needs of their partner in mind when resolving interpersonal issues. ***Imagine for a moment being less reactive during episodes of high emotional conflict.*** Then, imagine the possibility of ending your relationship and negotiating the terms of your settlement with kindness. Consider how this might reduce pain for both you and your partner, while increasing a positive sense of resolution for both parties.

Many of my clients confess they are better able to do this in business or with friends, but struggle to consistently extend compassion within their romantic relationships. The main point here is that the *capability* for compassion exists. It becomes harder to implement openness and compassion with those to whom we are more *attached* and thus *more vulnerable.* We simply have more at risk, emotionally speaking, the more intimate we are with

---

[1] (Kelly, Zuroff, and Shapira in 2009).

someone. But the capacity within us does exist. It is simply the effort or *practice* of extending compassion that is missing when we choose not to act from a place of compassion with our partner.

When we learn to regularly center ourselves in compassion, we are more capable of extending compassion to our partner in difficult moments. I have often seen that my clients who can pinpoint a specific "unforgivable act" or "pathological diagnosis" for their partner also struggle to find compassion for them. I most commonly see this when a client believes their partner is narcissistic (I believe this diagnostic term is inaccurately and grossly overused in our culture). In response to this, I greatly appreciate Brené Brown's conceptualization of narcissism from a perspective of vulnerability, which ultimately affords a position of increased compassion. For those of you not familiar, Brené is a renowned research professor at the University of Houston, made famous for her vulnerability presentation on Ted Talks. She has since authored many bestsellers on the subjects of courage, vulnerability, shame, and empathy. Viewing narcissism as a vulnerability, she explains it as the manifestation of shame from the fear of not being good enough, worthy, or loveable (Brown 2012). When considering narcissistic behavior from this lens, it is a bit easier to find compassion for the sometimes horrific behaviors and transgressions of a narcissist. We can instead understand that they are fearful and furious with the shame of feeling helpless. I share this example to illustrate that compassion is possible in all situations if we strive for it; and in order to achieve our post-divorce vision, we must learn to extend compassion in place of judgment.

Meditation Invitation: Fostering Vulnerability

It is through vulnerability that we find true strength and freedom, for in vulnerability we are our most authentic self. It is the practice of vulnerability that ultimately enables our compassion for self and others. Showing up as our authentic self leaves us with a sense of integrity in all that we do. Even when things do not go our way, we can rest in the knowledge that we were true to ourselves in each moment.

Retaining the vulnerable strength of the Heart Warrior within you is difficult at times, particularly in situations you may encounter during your separation or divorce. Being able to speak to your partner from a place of truth, without blaming, shaming, or making yourself a victim will aid you in finding your inner freedom and support your healthiest divorce process.

In this meditation exercise, find a quiet place to sit or lay down. Take three to ten full, deep breaths and let your body relax.

Once you have found a quiet space within, begin to repeat the following statements, along with any other statements that feel supportive and true to you:

"I accept myself fully, exactly as I am."

"I release any feelings of shame—I am good."

"I am enough. I am whole. I am worthy. I am lovable."

"I am safe and secure."

"I can keep myself safe."

"I am open to feeling whatever emotions arise."

"It is okay for me to have any feelings I experience."

"I am not my emotions."

"I do not need others' to approve of my emotions."

"I can speak my truth, even when it feels difficult."

At first, repeat three or more times any phrases that feel true and resonate for you. Next, try a few phrases that you would like to believe, but might not just yet. Repeat those phrases three or more times as well. Continue breathing and notice how you feel in your body as you move through this exercise and for a few minutes afterward.

To dive deeper into what compassion might look like: If my partner is doing the best they can in a given moment, and they are still unable to meet my expectations for love in the way I need, the problem is not only *my* personal experience of disappointment. Most likely, they are receiving my message that they are "not enough." *Being a disappointment to someone can be a shame-inducing experience.* So, at the very least, we might be able to extend compassion for how they feel receiving the message that they are failing us—even if our sentiment feels genuinely true in the moment!

Compassion is such an important part of a healthy divorce that it is next to impossible to have one without the other. It is very easy when something is ending to begin *blaming* your partner and yourself for your life not working out as you had hoped. It is also very easy during this time to become entrenched in *unhealthy guilt* or to its more damaging cousin, *shame.* Our judging, critical mind is a difficult trap to avoid, especially during times of grief. But, if we have any hope of a loving divorce, and for that matter, a healthy life, we must make efforts toward our commitment to compassion. *The first step in supporting our vision for a loving divorce is non-judgmental, compassionate acceptance of what we discover as we start to mindfully and honestly observe ourselves.* In addition to the exercise above, there are other exercises in the back of the book that will further help you cultivate compassion as a daily practice. If you want to test how compassionate you currently are, you may want to take Kristin Neff's online compassion quiz, which can be found on her website: self-compassion.org.

Chapter 4 Tools:

- Try to notice when you find yourself being judgmental or critical of yourself or your partner. Simply acknowledge that it has occurred and take note of how you feel. If you can recall a recent occurrence, jot it down in the space below along with a note of how you feel about it. Do not place judgment on yourself for recognizing this experience in yourself. Just hold the awareness that we are all human and extend compassion to yourself.

- Imagine yourself like a young child to practice being more compassionately understanding with yourself. Consider whether you would speak to a young child in the tone and manner in which you speak to yourself. Can you also imagine your estranged partner as a child? Does this allow you to be more compassionate with the way you think and interact with them? Perhaps considering the fears and pain they, too, struggle with might soften your heart toward them. In the space provided below, write down at least one topic about which you will work to be more compassionate with yourself.

You can find additional meditations for compassion on my website: DrRebeccaHarvey.com.

_____

_____

_____

_____

_____

_____

_____

_____

Chapter 5

Achieving Acceptance

"When something happens, the only thing in your power is your attitude toward it: you can either accept it or resent it."

– Epictetus

As we begin to practice compassion, both for ourselves and those around us, we may wish to focus more intently on *acceptance*. **Acceptance is the act of recognizing the reality of a situation without necessarily attempting to change it. It is not the same as agreeing with or liking the situation.** More accurately, when we accept, we stop trying to pretend, wish, deny, or change the situation at hand. Acceptance, coupled with compassion, will allow us to reduce the duration of our negative emotions as we accept our marital experience for what it is, rather than what we wish it was. This duo of acceptance and compassion helps us reduce "rumination" (repeatedly thinking about something, usually in a recurrent and unproductive manner) and instead use our thoughts for more productive thinking. We can then find empowerment to make purposeful choices in the areas where we can realistically make an impact.

Rumination, running a thought repeatedly through your mind, keeps you "stuck" in your painful thoughts. Rumination is the product of an untrained mind. When we ruminate, we repeat the same thoughts and scenarios over and over again, often in the unproductive hope of solving a problem or predicting an outcome to protect ourselves. We do this quite naturally. In fact, in some ways, this is what the brain is programmed to do—predict danger and protect us from pain to ensure our survival. Evolutionarily, it served a wonderful purpose, to keep us safe in times when we navigated dangerous terrain and cohabited with deadly wildlife. However, while these threats are no longer a part of our daily life, our brain still responds as if they are. Our brain does not understand the difference between physical and emotional pain. To the brain, pain is pain, and the brain wishes to avoid pain by finding logical solutions. Thus, it is important for us to learn to counteract our instincts so that we can control the inclination of our mind to ruminate. The examples to follow will demonstrate how you can begin to work on training your mind.

Mary frequently pictures frightening scenarios about how her divorce may play out or how life might turn out post-divorce, she is staying in a constant emotional state of anger, sadness, and fear. By doing this, she is wasting mental, emotional, and physical energy that could be used to build her new life and support herself in healthy ways. If she remains mentally spinning in rumination, she may not see her options to make wise choices—those which support a healthy outcome. However, if she consciously chooses to practice mindful acceptance and compassion, she will soon be able to see that her rumination is unhelpful. Thinking about our issues is only helpful in the service of making informative, necessary decisions. Let's face it, most of our spinning thoughts are unproductive fantasies of a future that will never take place, or memories of long-ago experiences from a past that no longer exists.

Mary will further discover that ruminating is upsetting, causing her to feel emotionally depleted or mentally distracted, with low energy, or physical illness. She can instead choose to practice the mindful method of accepting that the ending of a marriage is filled with uncertainty, as well as a myriad of accompanying positive and negative emotions. She can then extend kindness to herself, noting that she is doing her best during an inherently difficult process. This new approach may allow her to choose to operate from a place of compassion, by distracting herself when needed, seeking outside support, soothing herself with her own self-talk, or engaging in other healthy coping behaviors. With this approach, Mary can take care of herself by *refusing* to spend time *unproductively* thinking about upsetting things that create and perpetuate drama.

Using distraction as a coping skill, Mary might spend time engaging in a work task or hobby, such as reading or cooking, while deliberately choosing to place upsetting thoughts out of her mind. If this is too challenging, Mary might elect to seek outside support to distract herself from unproductive rumination. Support can be particularly helpful during times of emotional upset, and it can be obtained from various sources. Sometimes, it might be helpful for Mary to talk through thoughts and feelings with a trusted confidant. Other times, it might be nice to distract from upsetting emotions by doing something entertaining with someone she enjoys, refraining from discussing her current stress. Something that is always available to Mary is the option to speak kindly and reassuringly to herself. Using soothing self-talk is a habit we all need, regardless of our marital standing. To practice self-soothing, Mary could frequently remind herself that this difficult situation is temporary, she is doing the best she can, she can handle this challenge, and in the end, things will be better. These types of self-statements are all methods to move beyond upsetting emotion into a calmer emotional state.

As another example, if John begins speaking to himself in a critical and shaming manner, focusing on how he believes he is flawed, what he has done wrong, or how others might see him, he too creates a negative emotional state. This behavior of picking on himself creates no benefit for John. In fact, from this place of shame, he is significantly less likely to examine his unhealthy marital contributions in an effective way; instead, he only creates further emotional damage. This is because by shaming himself, he is activating the emotionally reactive part of his brain, rather than moving into the logical problem-solving area of his brain that could benefit him by promoting healthy insight. John would gain the most benefit by extending compassion for his mistakes and poor choices and then examining what he might wish to amend.

I often see clients treating themselves poorly in an expressed attempt to punish themselves into better behavior "next time." This NEVER works. Just like small children or pets, we will always perform and learn lessons best in a supportive, encouraging, and forgiving environment, because of this it is so important to keep that same mental environment with yourself.

Make a commitment to continually accept that there is nowhere to go to get away from your grief's pain. Instead, you must move through it to heal. When we refuse to accept this principle, we slow down or stunt our healing. Acceptance says, "Of course I feel sad when I consider ending my marriage; this is not how I'd hoped things would go." When we become fully present to the reality that even ending an unpleasant marriage can feel sad, we can then become fully present with our experience of sadness (i.e. tears, heavy or tight chest, sinking feeling, lump in our throat, etc.). We can allow the emotion to express itself physically until it is time for the emotion and accompanying sensation, or *feeling,* to move along. The important part here is that *we let it move along.*

Our emotions, like everything that exists, are just manifestations of energy. By its nature, energy wants to move. This energy is what we experience when we notice our "feelings." Feelings are the physical expression of our emotional energy. As research demonstrates, the energy of emotion can be released "somatically," or physically from the body, which allows our internal experience of the emotion to move on as well. Think of the way we experience the energy of negative emotions and how they are linked to a spectrum of illness and chronic or fatal disease, like headaches and ulcers on the lesser side, to heart attacks and strokes on the more serious side. In fact, scientific research shows a significant correlation between certain chronic emotional states and physical illness. For instance, cancer has been linked to depression, heart issues to anger, and gastrointestinal issues to anxiety, depression, anger, guilt, and shame. The scientific research supporting the connection between mind and body is so robust it builds a strong argument in favor of effectively managing your thoughts and emotions to support your physical well-being. The fact remains that we cannot avoid having negative emotions.

Many clients have told me that their goal is to "no longer have anger" or they wish to "always be happy." While this is a relatable and understandable hope, it is entirely unrealistic. The fact is, we cannot avoid our emotions no matter how evolved we may be. Emotions are a necessary part of life, and, what's more, they offer us rich and useful information about ourselves. *In fact, emotions are just messages, it is our job to listen and let them go on their way.* Our goal for emotional regulation is to learn to observe emotions, as they communicate to us through our physical *feelings*, determine what message they are relaying, and then allow them to move on. Our aim is to notice and respond to the messages without engaging in reactive behavior that is damaging to our bodies, lives, and relationships.

Feeling our negative emotions is a necessary part of the healing process. Whether you are literally letting go of your marriage or just letting go of what you had hoped your marriage would be in an effort to move forward into a healthier place, you must work through the emotions you experience. When we work to develop this skill of letting go, we feel more in control of our emotions, as we begin to recognize that our emotional discomfort is only temporary. In fact, ***emotions only last ninety seconds.*** Yes, while it may sound unbelievable, the physiological expression, or feeling of an emotion, takes ninety seconds to move through our brain and body. The neurochemicals associated with emotions create the feeling we experience. If we maintain an emotional feeling longer than ninety seconds, it is because we have chosen to do so by continuing to spend time dwelling on the thoughts that caused the emotion. We restart the ninety-second timer when we keep the emotions in our present moment rather than allowing them to move on. Most emotional experiences begin with our thoughts (conscious or unconscious) and end with our physical response. Even for those with anxiety patterns in which a physical sensation first triggers an emotional response, it is the thoughts they maintain in conscious awareness that perpetuate their experience. Believe it or not, the thoughts are our choice. The *temporary* sensations or feelings are the byproduct. We may not be able to stop the automatic thoughts and feelings, but we can take control of what we continue to spend time thinking about and thus feeling. Simply because you have a thought, does not mean it is true. *We create* ways of seeing the world to understand it and function in it. Those around us create their own understandings and see the world quite differently. Mindfulness can help you challenge the validity of your thoughts to assist you in letting go the thought and accompanying emotion. As I tell my clients often, if it is not a *productive* use of thinking, LET. IT. GO. The exercise to follow can assist you in learning to let go of your unproductive feelings.

Exercise Invitation:
Paradoxical Release of Anger

Just like all other emotions, anger is an appropriate emotion. Much of the time, anger is informing us about a boundary. Sometimes, we are angry because others have violated our boundary, and sometimes, we are angry because we have violated our own boundary by doing something we did not want to do. We usually do this to avoid another undesirable emotion, like guilt, hurt, or sadness. Anger itself is not bad. The way we choose to express our anger however, can be. We can learn to let go of anger.

In this exercise, close your eyes and allow something that angers you to come to mind. Start slowly, with something that rates at a 3 or 4 on a scale of 0-10, with 10 being most upsetting.

As you bring this feeling to mind, notice where you feel it in your body (i.e., jaw, stomach, fists). Next, imagine what color it might be, as well as what shape, size, and texture.

Bringing this image to mind will help you hold your focus on the sensation of the emotion. Allow yourself permission to feel your anger, without guilt, and do not analyze it as reasonable or unreasonable, for it does not matter for this exercise—focus only on the feelings.

Now say to yourself, "This is anger," or "I feel angry when I think about _____." Notice that it is possible to just feel your anger and not respond in an inappropriate manner.

Honor your experience of anger and practice having reasonable conversations with yourself, expressing your feelings without blame or defensiveness. For example, you may say, "I feel angry because I expected _____, and instead, I got _____." Or, "I feel very angry because I did not want to do _____, and I allowed myself to agree to it anyway." Or, "I feel furious because I told them not to do _____, and yet they did it anyhow."

After you have worked through a conversation or two in your mind, notice again the areas in your body where your anger resides.

Identify the color, shape, and texture of the feeling, and try to remain with the visual awareness for the next couple of minutes. You should notice the feeling subsiding within a couple of minutes if you will refrain from going back to the upsetting thought (recall the ninety-second rule). From this more relaxed place you can either distract yourself to another subject entirely or move on to cognitive interventions (from other exercises in this book) to work with your experience on a deeper level.

You can apply this same exercise to foster acceptance of any difficult feelings you are trying to work though. Remember not to judge what you find, but just notice and allow yourself space to create self-understanding. For example, "This is guilt (or sadness); I feel guilty (or sad) when I consider_____. I feel guilty (or sad) because _____."

Harvard-trained and published neuroanatomist, Jill Bolte Taylor, having suffered a stroke in the left hemisphere of her brain, reported on her discovery of the ninety-second rule in great detail. In her book, My Stroke of Insight (2008), she described the process by highlighting our 'response-ability,' defined as "the ability to choose how we respond to stimulation coming in through our sensory system at any moment of time." As Taylor explained, in under 90 seconds, the chemicals of an automatic emotional response are flushed from our blood stream. She detailed, "Once triggered, the chemical released by my brain surges through my body, and I have a physiological experience. Within ninety seconds from the initial trigger, the chemical component of my anger has completely dissipated from my blood, and my automatic response is over. If, however, I remain angry after those ninety seconds have passed, then it is because I have *chosen* to let that circuit continue to run [by thinking the thoughts or holding on to the 'storyline' that triggered the response in the first place, rather than returning to the present moment]." (Taylor 2008)

The storylines we create during life's situations lead us to attach a meaning to that situation thus having an emotional experience. In other words, we go through our days experiencing otherwise neutral situations, and attach a storyline to catalog what we have experienced. This is often the result of an assumption we are making, based on what we can see in the moment and our unconscious beliefs, developed from our previous life experiences. When we have had similar experiences repeatedly throughout life, we tend to derive similar meaning from them (i.e., people can't be trusted because everyone is selfish), and thus, we create similar emotional experiences for ourselves going forward (i.e., feeling anxious, angry, or fearful of others). Mindfulness helps us notice our belief patterns, challenge those beliefs, and leave space for a new understanding of situations and new ways of responding emotionally. Using the ninety-second rule helps us to accept what we are experiencing in the moment and challenge the storyline we may be engaging in. This will help us reach a state of emotional regulation.

During your consideration of divorce, separation, or mediation, you can fall back on this ninety-second rule to manage your emotions and greatly reduce emotionally based reactivity or impulsive responding. When we can allow emotions to settle before we respond, we are substantially more likely to respond in healthy ways that serve our end goal, rather than impulsively reactive ways that complicate conversations and perpetuate negative emotional states. The problem is if we don't know about the ninety-second rule it feels like our emotional state can only be resolved by reacting (i.e. saying exactly what is on our mind in the moment—which is usually less kind and tactful than what we might otherwise say).

Exercise Invitation:
Challenging Your Cognitions

Often, we take our thoughts at face value and perceive them as facts. From this place, we may feel righteous, or justified anger about a situation. To be clear, your thoughts are not facts. They are the opinions and experiences you have woven together to give you a shortcut for understanding the way the world operates. This is why people have such dramatically different beliefs and perspectives from one another. We can change our present emotional state by asking ourselves a very simple question, "Is my thought on this an indisputable fact with no other possible perspective if seen by a different person?" This does not mean "would my friends or neighbors share my opinion?" Rather would this, from every other possible perspective, be seen exactly as you see it now? Is it provable, undeniable, and written in stone?

Chances are, even if the situation could be seen as a fact in the operational details, it would not be seen as fact in an emotional interpretation of the situation.

For example, you would understand your ex's motivation behind their "bad" behavior differently than a neutral person (like the grocery store clerk) or your ex's friends or family. When we suspend judgement and stop operating as if we know all the answers and make all the rules, we may begin to soften our hard-lined stance of holding "the ultimate truth" above anyone else's truth. This expanded awareness can reduce our experience of righteous anger.

Working with your cognitions by challenging them allows you the option of softening your stance and allowing space for a difference of opinion or experience. When we can do this, we are more likely to release our grip on our anger, contempt, resentment, and even hurt feelings.

So it is with mindful awareness that we expand our practice of acceptance—we become aware of our emotions and the bodily sensations of their associated energy. We recognize the temporary nature of emotions so that we can learn to release the emotional energy in healthy and productive ways, all while keeping our post-divorce vision in mind. Remember that your objective during your divorce process is to maintain your sense of respect, uphold your values, and achieve a healthier, more peaceful life at the conclusion.

Chapter 5 Tools:

- Recall that acceptance is not the same as making something favorable or even okay. See if you can accept your reality as you currently see it, even if you don't like it. Can you be present with the emotion you might be currently experiencing and just allow it to be there, without attempting to change it? What message might it be giving you? Use the space below to brainstorm on this message.

- Recall that if we acknowledge the energy of an experience, we allow it to express itself and move on its way. The next time you have a negative emotion, sit with it for ninety seconds and watch how it shifts. Remember that you cannot reengage with your thoughts (or the storyline you created) about it or you will restart the ninety seconds.

- It is the ironic or paradoxical practice of refraining from attempts to change the emotion that allows space for it to express and move along. Can you practice sitting with your feelings for just a few minutes each day?

_____

_____

_____

_____

_____

_____

_____

_____

Chapter 6

Retaining Respect

"Respect is a two-way street; you've got to give it if you want to get it."

– RG Rich

Since one of the ways to support a healthy loving divorce is to uphold respect for both yourself and your partner, let's take a moment to explore this concept. Respect as a concept is understood in two basic ways. The first is having admiration or recognition of someone's abilities, qualities, or achievements. The second is consideration of or regard for others' feelings, rights, wishes, or perspectives. Both of these understandings of respect are necessary to achieve a healthy, loving divorce. The importance of respect during your divorce consideration and/or process comes into play in the way that you treat yourself and your partner.

We must remind ourselves of our *ability* to rise above reactivity and call upon our highest self if we hope to succeed in maintaining kindness. It is much easier to allow ourselves to be swept into the currents of emotion and fall into reactive behaviors and words. However, maintaining a feeling of respect for ourselves is much easier when we feel good about how we are engaging with those around us. Our respect for our right to be treated kindly and fairly support healthy boundaries and clear communication. We can embrace the belief that others are due respect regardless of who they are and how we feel about them.

Retaining Respect: Trevor's Story

When Trevor's wife told him she wanted a divorce, he was devastated. He did not want his marriage to come to an end and had come to therapy to work on himself in the hope of saving his relationship. During the process of therapy, he came to terms with his wife's decision and came to his own resolution to let go of their unhealthy marriage. Trevor worked through significant grief around the ending of his twenty-five-year relationship and the impact it would have on his family. At each decision point, he stayed focused on being as respectful as possible to the partner with whom he had built a life. When she was confused about her decision to divorce, he attempted to go to couples therapy. When she asked for additional time to make decisions, he attempted to give her space and slow down the pace of their divorce process.

Despite his wife's behavior seeming to lack consideration for him, he made considerable effort to maintain respect toward her, for Trevor was committed to a loving divorce process.

Eventually, with the divorce proceedings being dragged on by his wife's lack of cooperation and communication, Trevor attempted mediation. This required multiple attempts, as his wife continued to struggle with her decision, despite what appeared to be a favorable division of assets. Although he was frustrated with her behavior, Trevor maintained his commitment to being respectful. At some point during the divorce, due to his clarity that the marriage was over, Trevor decided to begin dating. Even in his decision to date, it was important to Trevor to respect his wife by not dating women in the area of town in which he previously went out with his wife. He also made a special effort to take his dates to places where he was certain he would not run into his wife or any mutual acquaintances.

> *Trevor's choices were not always easy, and his behavior toward his wife was not perfect. But for the most part, he did an exemplary job of remaining kind, loving, and considerate—despite his deep pain and sorrow about divorcing.*
>
> *Ultimately, by maintaining this commitment to respect, he ended his marriage feeling authentic and pleased with who he was throughout the process. His efforts at maintaining his integrity allowed him to move through his grief, own his negative contributions to the marriage, and be better prepared for a future relationship.*

In regard to your consideration of feelings, rights, and perspectives, you may not always agree with your ex. For that matter, you may not even like your ex, but you can choose to respect them as a human and honor their right to operate in the world in a way that likely differs from yours. It is easy to sit in a place of self-righteousness, but it is more important to respect that your journey is your own and your partner's is theirs. While you can share aspects of your journey together, you cannot dictate or control how your partner moves through their journey. If you make the decision that their choices for their journey prevent you from continuing to share your journey together, you can respectfully decline to move forward. And you can do this from a place of love and respect, without violating them with your words or actions. When you commit to being respectful, you energetically create an atmosphere of being treated with respect in return, whether by your ex or by the rest of the world.

Chapter 6 Tools:

- Take a moment to consider what behaviors would feel respectful or disrespectful to you. Using your tools of compassion, ask yourself: What behaviors would feel respectful versus disrespectful to your partner? Write these down in the space provided.

- What things might compromise your ability to maintain self-respect during your divorce process? Respect for your ex? Take a moment to consider or write out how you might avoid these pitfalls.

_____

_____

_____

_____

Exercise Invitation: Retaining Respect

This exercise is designed to help you consider what behaviors will support your best efforts to be respectful of yourself and your partner. Before important conversations, phone calls, or meetings, review this list. Use it as a gentle reminder of how you can bring about your post-divorce vision.

- *Try to listen with curiosity, rather than preparing your response in your own mind while your ex is speaking.*
- *Try to find some validity in your partner's response prior to sharing your point of view.*
- *Be aware of your facial expressions and body language. Try to keep them pleasant or neutral.*
- *Be careful to keep your tone kind and calm. Avoid condescending, annoyed, or otherwise rude tones.*
- *When you disagree, explain your position with "I" statements. Remember, your position is based on your opinion, your perspective, and your feelings...not a universal rule of how the whole world perceives things.*
- *Get comfortable with saying you're sorry when you have made a mistake or not been your best self.*

- *Speak to your partner as though they are intelligent (even if you do not believe they are).*

- *Consider compassion when trying to understand your ex. Try to remove them from the "calculating villain" role. Most people are not intentionally planning to cause you pain and suffering. Even if your partner was deliberately creating problems for you, choosing to view it as unintentional will leave you feeling better—since you have no control over their behavior either way.*

- *Refrain from criticizing, blaming, and shaming others. Phrase your statements remembering what is important to you rather than what they are not getting right.*

Chapter 7

Achieving Vulnerable Authenticity

"We are constantly invited to be who we are."

– Henry David Thoreau

Most of life's challenging experiences, like working on your marriage or navigating through divorce, require considerable strength and courage. Change can be difficult, and the mere contemplation of divorce can be quite scary, requiring a particular kind of courage. Finding your resilience to face the difficult decisions and emotions inherent in ending a marriage is undoubtedly challenging—as is trusting that you can build a new future if you leave your current life behind. The aspect of courage I wish to focus on here is the courage to be authentic and vulnerable in the midst of your divorce or consideration of divorce. I have had countless clients refer to their moments of vulnerability as feeling of "weakness," but in actuality, vulnerability is a significant act of strength. We are vulnerable when we take the risk to show all the way up— to be fully ourselves. Thus, vulnerability means allowing ourselves to operate from a genuine or authentic place of honesty as we maintain our commitment to our values (like being kind or peaceful, for example). These values and morals are likely those same guiding principles you used to create your post-divorce vision. When we are authentic, we rid ourselves of shame. Contrary to shame's sentiment that something is "wrong with us," authenticity demonstrates self-acceptance and sets the stage for increased compassion. Hiding who we are is at the root of much of our dysfunctional behavior, including codependency, poor boundaries, blame and attack behavior, criticism, and avoidance. As difficult as it may be, you will ultimately feel better about yourself if you allow your marital dissolution decisions to come from a vulnerable place of authenticity.

Exercise Invitation: Cultivating Courage

Fear is one of the most limiting emotions we can experience. While it is true that bad things can happen, we tend to exaggerate the unknown negative outcomes we fear. I love the ideas in psychologist and self-help author Dr. Susan Jeffers' book, Feel the Fear and Do It Anyway. When you're in a state of fear, she suggests, to examine the worst possible outcome and coach yourself through the reality that you would be able to handle it (even if you would hate for it to happen). By doing this, you can feel your fear about the unknown outcomes of various situations, but move forward despite the fear. In a situation like divorce, you will often be forced to move forward despite your fear surrounding your partner or the legal process.

In this exercise, you are asked to sit quietly with just one idea of something that is fearfully upsetting to you. As you hold this idea in your mind, take a deep breath into your belly and slowly let it out. Begin to repeat to yourself, "It is okay for me to feel frightened sometimes. I can handle difficult situations with ease. I am okay now. I will be okay then. This experience and this fear is temporary. I can trust myself to take care of myself and seek help when I need it." Then take another deep breath and let it all the way out. Imagine giving yourself a big hug. You've got this.

Authenticity is a sign of psychological maturity. Owning who you are without defensiveness or a need to distort reality demonstrates your authenticity. In fact, it is the lack of living authentically that brings most clients to my office. Though they are seeking solutions to addictive patterns, undesirable emotions, anxiety, depression, relational strife, and various disorders, a loss of authenticity is most often at the root of their issues. Authenticity, or being genuine to who we are, can also be described as living with integrity, or showing consistent honesty and adherence to our own personal values and morals. We sacrifice our authenticity for a number of reasons, often quite logical and well-thought-out reasons. However, the security we believe we are obtaining comes at the cost of silencing our beliefs, desires, and needs. In other words, if I go against my own values, morals, and guiding life principles, I ultimately sacrifice my integrity and lose my authenticity.

Vulnerability to show up authentically is the secret to connection and intimacy. Only when we are courageous enough to be fully honest about who we are in the depths of our being can we foster true connection. This is the importance of vulnerability. Authenticity, is our choice in each moment to be true to ourselves and allow others to see who we are. So, whether you attempt to reignite intimate connection through vulnerability in your marriage or make a commitment to move forward with your divorce to focus on building a future built on authenticity, vulnerability is the key to finding your wholeness.

Vulnerability and Authenticity: Lydia's Story

Lydia came to therapy for assistance with her divorce process. She and her husband had a seven-year marriage with a great deal of emotional upheaval. Their arguments escalated often and easily both within the marriage and during their separation.

Lydia was tired of fighting and was hoping therapy would help her reach a state of peace both in her mind and life in general. She expected this to be a challenge because her husband often came to her with a great deal of anxiety and big emotions, which felt overwhelming to her.

Additionally, at times, he consumed alcohol to the point of intoxication and during these times would call her to share his negative feelings or express his grievances. He would then call the next day when sober to apologize and try to have the conversation again, but still with big emotion. Lydia had a pattern of being guarded with her ex because she felt overwhelmed by his emotional expression. She would often shut down, becoming quiet and refraining from speaking to him at all. Lydia's goals for therapy were to become more in touch with her emotions, become better at expressing emotions, and be able to do so, even when others were disappointed by her feelings or disagreed with her perspective.

To uphold her goal of authenticity, Lydia worked in therapy to be courageous enough to tell her estranged partner that his behavior made it difficult for her to communicate clearly and openly with him. She explained that for their conversations to be productive there would need to be a scheduled time to talk, with planned topics of conversation, and a discrete time limit on the conversation. By sharing her boundaries and needs with her ex, she was expressing courageous vulnerability. In the future, when he engaged in this behavior, Lydia was able to tell him calmly that she was feeling overwhelmed by his volume and energy and needed to "press pause" and revisit the conversation at another time. Although this was difficult for her, she found that her ex would often calm himself down in order to continue the conversation with her. With this change, Lydia felt that she was heard and had an impact on her estranged partner leading to productive conversations. Lydia's courageous commitment to be vulnerable and authentic allowed their divorce process to become smoother and brought more peace to her life.

Chapter 7 Tools:

- Make a list below of what feels true and authentic for you in regards to what you need and desire for your life. For instance, are you seeking a more peaceful existence, or perhaps you are committed to being honest and operating with greater integrity in your life. Maybe you want to get back in touch with the joyful, laughter-filled part of yourself.

- After making your list, consider and jot down how you might support those goals in a practical manner. For instance, if you want to be more honest with others, you may need to practice by taking a brief moment to reflect and consider how to proceed, prior to responding to questions asked of you.

- Can you find a respectful way to honor these needs, or, if necessary and appropriate, share them with your estranged partner? For example, "Because I am committed to maintaining greater peace in my life, I will not be engaging in hostile interactions and will be taking a time-out any time we enter a space of hostile communication." Or, "I am really working to be more honest, which is difficult for me when I believe I will upset someone with the truth. So, I may need to take a little space prior to answering your questions and appreciate you having patience with me."

_____

_____

_____

_____

_____

_____

_____

Chapter 8

Sustaining Self-Care

"To love oneself is the beginning of a lifelong romance."
– Oscar Wilde

Intentional self-care is something I advocate regularly to my clients and something I personally do each day. Self-care is the act of supporting your health emotionally, mentally, and physically. There are many ways you can care for yourself, including how you speak to yourself, who you spend time around, and how you honor your boundaries. But I'd like to focus on your behaviors and the activities you engage in to maintain your healthiest version of you. When you are your healthiest you, you will make better, more authentic choices and respond in ways according to your desired outcome.

> *Our psyche pulls us toward presence and health, and once there, it finds peace through greater emotional balance.*

One way to increase peacefulness in our lives is to begin and end each day with a commitment to our post-divorce vision and our general personal wellness goals. For many, personal wellness will include remembering this is a temporary life experience, taking personal inventory, or finding moments of spiritual connection. There are many ways to obtain spiritual connection such as through prayer, meditation, contemplation, or recitation of scripture or mantra. Keeping a gratitude journal is another powerful way to support yourself spiritually and keep your mind in a positive place. Practicing gratitude increases dopamine in your brain. Dopamine is the neurotransmitter associated with feeling good. When you receive this dopamine release, your brain will naturally want to seek more things to be grateful for and thus receive more dopamine. In time, a "feel good feedback loop" is created. You may find listening to scripture or encouraging music or reading supportive quotes is helpful for you. However, these are not the only ways to reconnect with your goals for a healthy life. Regardless of the method you choose, it is important to find what is important to you and what supports you in being the best version of yourself. A few exercises to support yourself spiritually can be found on the following pages. This includes a meditation, a visualization, and how you can use a gratitude journal.

Spiritual Exercises
(Cultivating Compassion and Love)

If you are spiritual, your relationship with your higher power can provide support and facilitate tremendous growth. Engaging in daily rituals of prayer, meditation, contemplation, or scriptural reading can provide peace of mind and increase faith and hope for the future.

In times of high emotional arousal, rumination or fixation on particular thoughts can occur. Use of spiritual practices can assist you in letting go of unproductive thoughts and help you focus on positive and supportive thoughts. Spiritual practice offers you peaceful moments, assists with forgiving your partner, and facilitates the release of your pain. It is also a surefire way to cultivate compassion for yourself and others. It's worth mentioning that simply asking your higher power to help you let go of negative feelings and replace those thoughts with well wishes can change the way you feel in your body and mind, which will likely change the way you engage with your ex.

If you are open to it, now is perfect time to start using prayer, meditation, or visualization each day to release your negative emotions and substitute them for positive, uplifting emotions. ***Keeping a journal is a particularly good way to process through your feelings and track which types of prayer, scripture, or visualizations are helpful.***

Keep in mind the spiritual principal of ten. This says that whatever we put into the universe comes back to us tenfold.

Deciding what you want to cultivate in your own life is supported by sending that desired energy to your ex. You can engage in various lovingkindness meditations or visualizations of blessing your partner (as well as anyone else you wish to include).

Meditation Invitation: Lovingkindness

One of the easiest ways to do a lovingkindness meditation is to imagine the person in your mind and repeat the words "lovingkindness." Lovingkindness meditation is a way to foster compassion for your ex. Not because they have earned it in any way, but simply because they are, just as you are, a living soul.

Visualization Invitation: God's Eyes

In this exercise, I ask you to imagine your higher power as though they are standing with you or surrounding you—witnessing your thoughts, words, and actions.

Now imagine your ex is standing in front of you and imagine seeing them through God's eyes (whatever "God" may be for you). This may be difficult, especially if visualizing is hard for you. But recall the infinite forgiveness, compassion, hope, and love God has for us all (and try to

If you find this too difficult, you can think of the love an idealized mother or father would have for their child. Let this idea of unconditional love guide how you see your ex.

Exercise Invitation: Radical Gratitude

While it may seem impossible to think of the things you are grateful for about your ex, it is possible. The Bible says, "In all things be grateful." In Judaism, there are blessings to show gratitude for everything: the food we eat, the air we breathe, seeing a rainbow. Even mundane things are worthy of gratitude. A traditional Islamic saying states, "The first who will be summoned to paradise are those who have praised God in every circumstance."

A few years ago, I was inspired by my mother. In a very public social media movement, she embarked on her goal to spend a year documenting 1,000 things she was grateful for. It took a few months as she moved through the low-hanging fruit of the more obvious positives, but I soon began to see things like, "I'm grateful for my alcoholic father," and "I'm grateful for difficult marriages."

*I then understood her goal was to find gratitude in **everything**, even the painful parts of her life, as she could now see how they shaped her.*

When I reflect on my own life, I am ultimately grateful for the lessons I learned, however difficult the lesson was at the time. In fact, once I have gained some distance and have a new perspective.

I'm thankful for all of my struggles, failed projects, and relationships. Thinking of my mother's year-long project and my past experiences, I decided, If I know I'll be grateful for this experience one day, why not embrace it now for the benefits and guidance I cannot yet see?

So this is what I do. I now follow her lead and try to find gratitude in all moments, even the less desirable ones. Believe me, it is hard. Sometimes very, very hard. But I always feel better—comforted by the idea that this is all working to my greater good.

For your practice, each morning (and/or night) write down three things about your life with your ex-partner that you are grateful for. Easy ones might be for your children, learning to salsa dance, or your happy memories. Harder ones might include discovering that you are codependent, learning to stand up for yourself, or becoming more financially aware as you separate finances. Use the space below to get started. **Remember, you can find gratitude in everything!**

The simplest way to support myself each day is by first reserving time for myself for the specific purpose of providing self-care. Secondly, I ask myself, "What do I need right now?" Sometimes, what I need is not available to me in that moment. However, acknowledging what I need brings it to the forefront of my awareness and hopefully allows me to meet that need in some partial way or address it at a later time. For instance, there are times when I am feeling tired, and, as I check my energy levels, I am immediately aware that my body wants to slow down and take a nap to recharge. Often this occurs in the midst of a busy workday when this is clearly not an option. In these cases, I might try to lay down for the five minutes I have between clients, set a gentle alarm, and just allow myself to "nap" for that short duration. While it does not give me the full reset of a nap, I do benefit both from the act of honoring my needs (as opposed to denying them) as well as from giving myself a small dose of what I need. It's like having a snack when you're starving. You will still need to eat a full meal at some point, but the snack temporarily satisfies.

Acknowledging our needs is a way to love and honor ourselves and keep us in touch with our unfolding life experience. I have met many people who have ignored their needs and thus neglected themselves for much of their lives. Honoring our experience by acknowledging it fully brings us personal insight and a sense of empowerment, even when our options for action are limited by life circumstances. I have yet to see someone who's become more present in their life later wish to return to a state of disconnect and denial. It is my belief that our psyche pulls us toward presence and health. Once there, it helps us find peace through greater emotional balance.

Personally, I create time both in the morning and at night to check in with what I need. During my divorce process, I increased my self-care by committing to daily "rituals" (a combined series of healthy behaviors) I knew to be most helpful for releasing emotions, recharging myself, and supporting my best mindset. For me, this included meditation and prayer in the morning, followed by oil pulling for thirty minutes (an Ayurvedic practice of swishing oils in the mouth that is believed to pull toxins from the body), which I did while I silently performed my morning chores, like feeding my dogs and making breakfast. Both of these behaviors allowed me an extended period of silence in which I could not and did not converse with anyone. This helped to create balance in my high energy personality and my highly conversational career. During this time, I would check in with myself by asking, "What do I need?" while scanning my body, my energy levels, and my emotional state. This question led me to decide how to spend my remaining morning time prior to work (i.e., yoga, gardening, reciting affirmations, going for a run or bike ride, or walking my dogs). On the following pages you will find an exercise to guide you through affirmations as well as an incredibly powerful meditation I used often during my divorce.

> ### *Exercise Invitation: Daily Affirmations*
>
> *Our thoughts and self-talk are incredibly powerful. Sometimes, we move through our days using negative affirmations, saying things like, "I'm so stupid," or "I'm never going to get this right." When we do this, we are limiting our reality and creating a low energetic vibration that does not serve us in any way and leaves us feeling depleted. Finding positive affirmations is relatively easy and sets your mood and mindset for the day (or night). You can find ideas for your personal affirmations on the internet or in the many books that exist on the topic. One of my favorite authors is self-help healer Louise Hay—she also has several online resources, including free recordings you can listen to in the background during your morning or evening routines. The trick to your positive affirmation is that you must say it as if it is already true...whether or not you believe it.*

By stating it as if it is already true, you are creating the space for it to be true, through visualizing it and experiencing it, which will support your best possible outcome.

For this exercise, you are asked to engage in this behavior as much as possible, but at least in the morning or at night.

It doesn't take much time and since you're already talking to yourself all day, anyway, you may as well use mindful awareness to attend to what you're saying and turn it into a positive affirmation. It is a good idea to repeat positive affirmations several times over—at least three times. An example of this is: "My divorce is working out in the best possible way for all parties." You can use this any time you notice anxiety or discomfort arising in your divorce process. Using the space below, write out some affirmations that would be uplifting to you.

_____

_____

_____

_____

_____

_____

Meditation Invitation: Blessing Circle

Imagine drawing a large circle and placing inside that circle everyone who carries emotion surrounding your divorce. This will obviously include your ex and yourself. You may also want to consider adding his or her attorney, family members, friends, the person with whom he or she was unfaithful (no, I'm not joking), or even your children if you have any divorce-related negative feelings. Anyone who has contributed or sustained emotions around your divorce can be placed in this circle—and the circle may change slightly from day to day (but will always include you and your partner).

Now the task becomes trickier. Your goal is to send blessing and forgiveness to each person, as well as love, prosperity, peace, happiness, joy, success, understanding, compassion, and any other positive attribute you can imagine. You may notice resistance as you do this but keep with it!

You can imagine sending these qualities from your heart in the form of light or brightly colored smoke, or my favorite option—liquid. Any liquid form you can imagine (water, paint, bubbles...) from any source (rain, a bubble gun, a hose...) will work. You should envision completely covering (or soaking) the person in light, smoke, or liquid, filled with happiness, blessings, and forgiveness.

You will continue to focus on each individual until you see that person smiling back at you (I learned this last bit from a spiritual intuitive, Gary Berman's visualization workshop and found that it was a true test of whether I had released negativity if I could allow myself to see the person smiling back. So please don't skip this part). This exercise can be a difficult but powerful experience. It will literally change the feeling in your body when you think of the previously upsetting individual. Do not forget to include yourself each time you do this exercise!

In addition to the self-care behaviors that I adjust according to my needs, there are other behaviors I strive to implement daily. Across ample research, certain factors emerge as having the most significant impact on the maintenance of our basic mental health. There are three factors which, when combined with regularity, dramatically stand out in their contribution to our ability to maintain a healthy, balanced mood. I refer to these factors as "The Big Three."

The Big Three include:

1. Sleeping for 7 to 9 hours per night (or 7 to 8 hours if you are over 64 years of age)

2. Eating a healthy breakfast each morning

3. Exercising for at least 30 minutes a day

Breakfast does not need to be a large, heavy meal, but rather needs to "break the fast" of our previously non-nourished time period. Further, our exercise (for this purpose) does not need to be vigorous, but might be a slow-paced walk around the block. The important thing is that these three behaviors together help to regulate and/or reset various systems of the body—circulatory, digestive, and nervous, among others. We need The Big Three for our general well-being. Sadly, it is usually these three factors that fall off our plate as soon as we become stressed or "too busy." Without fail, this is one of the pieces of information I gather at a client's initial visit to my therapy office. If these are not being achieved, this is the first place we start. It is amazing how much more manageable our life decisions become when we are armed with The Big Three.

With the stress of your divorce consideration or process, it may be more difficult to stay focused on The Big Three. It is important to realize these, like all other recommendations in this book, are *guidelines*; goals to work toward. Stressing yourself out for not obtaining them with perfection and consistency defeats their purpose. DO YOUR BEST. If you only have time for 5–10 minutes of exercise while you walk your dog, that is better than not exercising at all. If you only get 6 hours of sleep, try to find a time to grab a little more in the next couple of days. Again, the goal of this is to improve your emotional climate and thus support a better mood. So, be kind to yourself as you attempt to increase attention to any of the suggestions in this book.

Creating a plan for activities of self-care is an important part of supporting yourself mentally, emotionally, and physically during your time of separation or divorce. You will want to create a schedule and a list of tasks that are reasonable and realistic for you to complete on a daily/weekly basis. It is important during this time (and always) to do *things that feel good,* activities you enjoy or that leave you with an improved mood or in a more resilient emotional state. It may take time for you to decide which activities will best suit your immediate needs and which will fit into your life in an ongoing capacity. But if you take time to create this plan, you are more likely to follow through with it and will certainly feel more stable during your separation or divorce process. Examples of self-care behaviors and assistance with creating your personal self-care plan can be found on the following page.

Chapter 8 Tools:

• Take a moment to consider how you speak to yourself when you are feeling stressed or in a low mood. Is there anything you would like to change about it?

• Instead of being harsh or discouraging with yourself, ask yourself, "What do I need right now?" Write down your answers in the space provided. Can you attempt to give some aspect of that to yourself?

• Take a moment to consult the Self-Care Planning Guide below and make a list of things you can do periodically to find a moment of joy or leave yourself feeling recharged.

• If you don't already, consider implementing The Big Three as often as you can. Strive to get 7 to 9 hours of sleep, exercise daily, and have breakfast each day.

_____

_____

_____

_____

_____

_____

_____

Self-Care Planning Guide

When developing your self-care plan, there are a few important considerations. To begin, it is important to find things you can implement in your daily life that are not going to create additional stress or cause guilt if you're unable to complete them. The idea is to choose things that are simple and accessible—easily repeatable behaviors are important. Something you can sustain or add to a routine would be ideal. Lastly, try to make it affordable.

In other words, you might be able to take a trip to Europe as "self-care," but this grand gesture might cause financial strain and is not something you can easily call upon when you are in need of a stress break. You want to be sure your plan for self-care is always available, rather than having to put forth a great deal of effort when you need it.

Self-care is about what you need in the moment. If you typically go for a run to decompress, but on a given day you feel exhausted and sense a nap would better serve you, be sure this flexibility is built into your plan.

The last thing you need is to feel guilty about forgoing your run for a nap—that will only add stress to your life. That is not to suggest that we will always want to expend the energy of exercising to obtain the benefits, but when you truly sense your body and energy levels need something else, listen to your instincts!

Social contact is another important consideration in self-care. While solitude can be helpful and meet some needs, it's quite easy to move into a space of habitual isolation, which can create loneliness and contribute to mental, emotional, and physical health difficulties. Pay attention to your instincts. You might feel like isolating yourself in response to your low mood, but remember that simple actions like a phone call with a friend or joining a social group might be a more supportive exercise.

Below is a list of self-care activities; there is no way I could list all of the various options available to you. But hopefully, some of these ideas will work for you or spark another activity or behavior that will fit. Use the space provided below to write down your favorite self-care ideas and use this to formulate your plan.

Self-Care Ideas

- Develop a sleep routine
- Eat breakfast each day
- Go for a walk
- Play fetch with your dog
- Drink water
- Take an art class
- Take dance lessons
- Sing/Listen to music
- Play an instrument
- Journal your thoughts
- Read a book
- Engage in a favorite hobby
- Start a new hobby
- Garden
- Do a craft project
- Visit a museum
- Sit in a park
- Go on a picnic
- Go swimming
- Get some sunshine
- Take your kids somewhere fun
- Take your dog to the park
- Leave inspirational quotes around your house
- Play

_____

_____

_____

_____

_____

_____

_____

Chapter 9

Building Healthy Boundaries

*"Boundaries are the distance at which I can
love me and you simultaneously."*

– Prentis Hemphill

Another specific way can we take care of ourselves is by having healthy boundaries. Our boundary recognition and implementation is an important aspect of emotional regulation. Healthy boundaries nourish healthy relationships, including the one you have with your partner or ex-partner. It is so important, in fact, that the topic deserves a book all its own. Boundaries will be discussed here briefly to help you make responsible choices about how you engage with your partner. It may be that boundaries were a problem in your marriage, and regardless of your decision to stay or leave your marriage, now is a wonderful time to begin working on them. While you and your partner may have had difficulty recognizing, expressing, or holding your boundaries, you will most certainly benefit from dedicating some attention to them now. Doing so will not only shift the interactions between you and your partner but will also improve your feelings about yourself as you become clearer about your needs and limits. Clearer boundary awareness allows you to be more effective with your emotional regulation. Additionally, if you choose to end your marital relationship, having healthy respect for and navigation of boundaries will assist you in selecting and supporting any future relationships, romantic or not.

Take a moment here to consider how you are managing your personal boundaries. Do you say yes when you really mean no? Do you take care of others' needs at the cost of meeting your own needs? Do you often find yourself angry as you agree to go along with someone's requests, when you'd rather not? Your consideration of others is a wonderful thing, but it may work against you with regard to having healthy boundaries. As self-help author and codependency guru Melody Beattie shares in her book of daily meditations, *The Language of Letting Go,* "We cannot simultaneously set a boundary and take care of another person's feelings. It is impossible, as the two acts contradict" (Beattie, 1990). Once this is understood, many of us quickly become aware of the boundaries we have been ignoring.

When I am working with therapy clients on their boundary navigation, there is a sort of "pendulum swing" that occurs as those who have not been setting boundaries begin to recognize and assert them. That is to say, I often see clients who have habitually "gone along" with what others want— or worse, allowed others to treat them like a doormat— begin setting boundaries in an excessively aggressive manner to communicate their limits. It is as if they are "clunking" someone over the head when they deliver the message that a boundary exists. In their effort to swiftly communicate their boundary message, they respond in harsh tone, sharp words, or outbursts of anger.

A strong expression of anger is a quick and easy way to communicate and uphold a boundary. However, the very real fact is that it is reasonable for others to ask us for their needs and wants, just as it is reasonable for us to ask for what we want and need. In fact, it is incumbent upon each of us to communicate our desires and our limits, when appropriate.

The goal of boundary work with a partner, or anyone else, is to express our needs and limits in the kindest way *with the least amount of force*. I work with my clients to help them understand that there are levels to how they assert/enforce their boundaries. While some people respond easily to the subtle suggestion of a boundary, others require a direct but cordial communication, and still others need a very firm and explicit communication. If none of these preliminary approaches is effective, a "clunk" is the last resort and tends to work quickly with most people. This is because expression of anger is easily perceived and thus grabs the recipient's attention, whether it be frustration, irritation, annoyance, or rage. However, problems occur when we go directly to "clunking" without attempting the kinder, gentler option. By doing this, we cultivate anger in ourselves as a general state of being, and the result is that others tend to fear us (or tiptoe around us). Another result of us using "clunking" too quickly is that people learn to approach us with a preemptive defensive stance, prepared to battle us when disagreement arises, which on our end feels like an unprovoked attack. In other words, we can feel attacked by others simply because they are approaching us expecting that *we* are planning to be aggressive. As you can see, going too quickly to a "clunk" does not support a kind and collaborative interaction with your partner or anyone else.

Boundary levels can be explained by what I affectionally named the "One, Two, Three Clunk Theory." I named this theory after a supervisory experience with Dr. Fiona Chalom, many years ago in my doctoral program at Pepperdine. One day, during case consult, she shared the concept of levels existing in our assertion of boundaries. I quickly donned and later expounded the concept of "boundary levels" to coach my own clients as they work to navigate the sometimes confusing terrain of boundaries.

Boundary Levels

The way I explain boundary levels in a simple scenario is this: If you bring a plate of cookies and set it on the table in front of me as you offer me a cookie, you are expressing your desire to share your cookies. If I refrain from taking one as we continue our visit, I have subtly communicated that I am not interested in a cookie, and, if I did want one, we can assume

*I would have taken you up on your offer by taking a cookie. This subtle exchange is what I call a **Level One Boundary**. Many people "miss" a Level One Boundary altogether. Further, you may have a strong desire for me to have one of your cookies and thus, may invite me again to take cookie.*

*At this point, I might elect to move from a level one to a **Level Two Boundary** as I communicate: "That's so kind of you, but I'll pass on a cookie right now." This more cordial response is kind and pleasant, but clearly, I state that I do not plan to eat a cookie. Keep in mind that offering a "reason" for not taking a cookie (i.e., I am not eating sugar, or I am full) is not necessary, but discretionary. In fact, sometimes, offering a reason sets us up to be challenged by the other person.*

*When anyone, including your partner, is preoccupied with their own needs or wants, they will press on despite the kind and clear communication of a Level Two Boundary. In these moments, a **Level Three Boundary** is needed.*

> *Level Three might drop the pleasantries and simply, firmly express the intent: "I don't want a cookie," or "I'm not going to eat a cookie." This communication couldn't be any clearer. Notice that none of these three responses resulted in a lengthy explanation in which I tried to get you to like my choice, agree with me that I shouldn't eat a cookie, or attempt to change your mind about wanting me to have a cookie. Your wants and needs are your own. **We do not need someone to like, understand, or agree with our boundaries.** They are ours.*

Many people assert their boundaries at one of the levels and then give in when pressed. Others stop short in their communication before the cookie sharer has clearly been given the boundary message and instead go straight to a "clunk" after the first offer of a cookie. This would certainly feel confusing and unreasonable to someone who simply wants to share their baked goods! Imagine how awful it might feel if you were the one attempting to share your cookies and were "clunked" or treated with aggression in response. In this cookie scenario, I simply hold my ground that I do not plan to eat a cookie. If my communications are ignored and you continue to pressure me to take a cookie, *this* is a perfectly reasonable time to allow my irritation to show. I might say, "Enough with the cookies, I'm not having one!" It's not necessary for me to throw the plate of cookies across the room, though that would surely express my stance. It is also not necessary to criticize, shame, or read into your motives for offering me cookies with a personal attack on you. An example of an attack response would be: "You're such a jerk, always trying to get me to eat cookies. You must want me to be diabetic!" Without personal attack or excessive aggression, I can simply say, "No."

Your needs will be different than others' needs, including those of your partner or ex-partner, and that is okay. Neither of your needs to be "wrong" for having your own desires or needs. Couples often get side-tracked here, moving into a debate of whose needs are "reasonable." In fact, some clients question why I wouldn't have just taken the cookie to be kind, but then not eat it. That is an option (and in some unique situations, it might be appropriate), but it's certainly a confusing response, as serving myself implies that I will be eating the cookie. When you are later asked if you enjoyed the cookie, this misleading response results either in further deception by reporting on a cookie you never ate, or hurt feelings, when someone realizes they have been deceived by your actions. For the purposes of being authentic and keeping our integrity, it is simpler to be clear about our limits and allow ourselves to sit in the discomfort of difference. With regard to boundaries, less is more, until more is required. Try to learn to communicate with your partner in a manner that is respectful, but clear.

One thing to keep in mind in difficult situations is that *proximity boundaries* are the simplest to uphold. Taking physical space from one another can reduce or prevent a lot of issues. When in doubt, take physical space and allow some time between your feelings and your response to your partner. You can always offer to "think something over" and get back to them, even if they prefer an immediate response. You have the right to take space as a way of honoring your boundary—whether it's five seconds, five minutes, or five days. Keep in mind that it is okay for others to disagree with and be disappointed in our choices, which can happen when we are attempting to take care of ourselves.

When dealing with your partner, there will certainly be boundaries to navigate for both of you as you attempt to move through the decisions in your divorce process. We all have different and uniquely personalized boundaries. Your boundaries may be very different from your partner's, but they still deserve respect. Learning to respect your partner's boundaries, in addition to your own, will serve you well and reduce frustration. Learning to communicate yours (and uphold them) will also serve you well in your other relationships, by reducing the emotional upheaval of misunderstandings and taking the guesswork out of communication.

Remember, a foundational aspect of boundaries is that you *do not need to explain them*. Often, we choose to do so with the hope of creating agreement or understanding or to reduce negative feelings for one or both people. We try to make upholding our boundaries "easier." However, explaining your reasons for your boundaries can be a slippery slope that might place you in a position of "asking permission for" or "negotiating" your boundaries. In navigating boundaries with a separate marital partner, the feeling that you *need* your partner understand or agree with your

require agreement nor understanding from other person to be completely appropri[ate], healthy, and upheld you as such.

boundaries can result in a conversation that challenges your logic or rationale for having the boundary. This type of conversation opens you up to the possibility of being coerced or manipulated into changing your position or going against your boundaries to please the other person—which may not serve *your* best interests. If you truly need to talk through your boundaries during this time, it would be best to do so with a trusted therapist or friend.

Boundaries Aren't Negotiable:
Marie's Story

Marie arrived to therapy frustrated. She witnessed her estranged husband Mark to be controlling and manipulative, and she felt depressed and unable to stop his behavior. After discussing a few specific situations, it was clear Marie was not holding her boundaries with Mark. She would often engage in conversations with her ex in which he would question her reasoning for the decisions she made and then persuade her, with persistence, to "see things his way."

After these conversations, she would often end up doing things as Mark wished. Sometimes, she did this to avoid a more significant argument or because she felt guilty that he was disappointed with her choices. On other occasions, she second-guessed her choices because she had always perceived Mark to be "very intelligent—smarter than me."

Regardless of her reasoning, Marie consistently felt angry that she was not making healthy choices for herself, and she felt she couldn't escape Mark's control. This left her feeling unprepared for life after her marriage, while still wishing she could escape Mark. Marie got help through therapy. She looked to improve her boundary awareness and her comfort with holding her boundaries so that she could simultaneously increase her sense of self-esteem and learn to take care of herself post-divorce. Most significantly, Marie learned to communicate her choices to Mark and refrain from automatically answering all of his questions about her decisions. Marie's ability to discern when to answer his questions and when to simply inform him of her choices improved their communication significantly and gave Marie the needed confidence to move forward with her divorce.

A special consideration must be made for setting limits with those who are emotionally immature, abusive, or enjoy conflict, as this can prove particularly challenging. An emotionally immature person can have a distorted sense of reality, struggle to accept responsibility for their actions, believe the universe revolves around them, or have problems upholding their commitments. Attempting to engage in healthy communication with these individuals or make rational decisions together can prove next to impossible. This situation would be best supported by a therapist and may require individualized coaching to support you in your commitment to divorcing in love. In the words of Marianne Williamson (1992), "Whether we choose to focus on the guilt in their personality, or the innocence in their soul is up to us." Regardless of what you may be dealing with or how difficult you may find your ex to be, you can still move toward the most peaceful and loving divorce process possible, even when your partner is not on board. Your healthy choices to this end, like your boundaries, *do not require agreement or understanding from the other person to be completely appropriate and healthy.* The exercises on the following page are helpful to disentangle yourself from being pulled into the chaos of an emotionally immature person. These exercises can help you remember the emotional boundaries that exist between you.

Visualization Invitation: Not Mine

Sometimes, we get pulled into other people's emotions. This is especially true for highly sensitive people, or empaths, and for those of us still working to overcome codependency. It is important to recognize when you are being pulled into someone else's emotions and learn to create an emotional boundary to separate their feelings from your own. We all have the right to our feelings, and as long as we are not being abusive or intrusive with others, we have the right to feel our feelings as we see fit. Allow others the space to feel their feelings and yourself the space not to join them. Sometimes, other people will want you to join in their emotion with them (or for them) and may be upset when you decline the invitation to join them. This is okay. They may fuss or even temper tantrum and that is also okay. You do not need to respond to other's dissatisfaction in those moments.

When you feel yourself being pulled into someone else's emotional experience or find yourself thinking negatively about someone, I suggest one of two options.

I have come across versions of this from various books and energy healers. The idea is to disconnect your energy from the other person's energy. The first option is simply saying out loud, "This is not mine. Get out!" and imagine physically taking the emotion from your body and tossing it out. This is a great way to manage rumination on unproductive negative emotion that exhausts your time and energy resources.

However, my favorite version of this exercise is a gentler approach that leaves me feeling better inside. I imagine the emotion, take a deep breath into the space I feel it in my body, and then imagine breathing it out as I send it back to the other person, saying, "I send this back to you with consciousness and love." This last practice leaves me feeling peaceful and loving. The truth is, if the feeling is not mine, there is nothing for me to do with it, and the other person needs to deal with it on their own.

Visualization Invitation: Cutting the Cord

I credit this exercise to an energy healer from Hawaii named Hannah Taua. The point of the exercise is to disconnect your energetic or emotional ties from another person. It is designed to reduce the emotional impact they have on you and to reduce your upset in situations involving them. Hannah instructs that this exercise be done three times, once per day over three consecutive days and then repeated once a week for the next four weeks.

As she instructs, first, you visualize a cord running from your belly button to your ex-partner's or the situation you are trying to disconnect from. If you cannot visualize it, you can say out loud, "I see a cord running from my belly button to [your ex's name]." You can also include any other people or situations with which you are struggling. You then imagine grabbing that cord and "dramatically" pulling it out of your belly button while you say, "I'm pulling that cord off of me."

Then dramatically throw it down and say, "In that hole, I place golden light," as you visualize placing a little ball of golden light into your belly button. Then tap your belly three times, and you're done.

I use this exercise as often as necessary when I feel a need to detach. I love this exercise because it offers something spiritual and intentional to do with the lingering feelings and thoughts of your ex. It does not require you to never see them again or think poorly of them, but you are detaching your energy...with love.

An additional area of boundary consideration is how you will set boundaries with family, friends, and others as you consider or move through your divorce. It is important to think about how much you will share and with whom. Because it is crucial that you feel supported during this time, you may want to consider how a therapist could assist (with no outside accountability to your social circle). You may find you need increased support from trusted loved ones, such as a close friend or family member. But consider your relationship vision and how your decision to share could impact your future. Be particularly cautious in considering who will be likely to spread the personal information you share. For instance, some might hold their own grudges toward your ex, that could later interrupt your healing process or negatively influence your post-divorce vision once *you* have forgiven and moved forward. You may feel a need to vent to your friends and family for support. But, once the "dust has settled," it is those same friends and family that may continue to be unkind to your ex in social settings or say negative things to you—long after you have softened your heart and forgiven your ex.

It is also important to note how your estranged partner might feel about what you share, as this is also their personal information. You may feel in this moment or some later moment that you "don't care" how your ex feels about what you share. This is precisely when you will want to refer to your post-divorce vision and call upon qualities previously discussed, like compassion, acceptance, respect, and authenticity.

Lastly, I would encourage you to refrain from sharing information with your children, other than what is essential for their understanding and ability to process the situation. They do not benefit from being kept completely in the dark, but they certainly suffer when they are overly involved in adult matters, such as your thoughts and feelings about your estranged or damaged relationship. If you are unclear about what is appropriate to tell your children, I suggest speaking to a professional, or at least consulting a book written by a professional, to help you walk this difficult path. Much like you, your children need healthy support to get through this difficult experience.

Chapter 9 Tools:

• Take an inventory of how healthy your boundaries are at present. How often do you say "yes" when you really mean "no"?

• How might you express your boundaries in the kindest way, while still remaining firm? In what ways might you be "negotiating" your boundaries by offering unnecessary information or reasons for your choice? It feels good to be understood, but it is not necessary regarding our boundary work, and may serve to complicate our efforts.

• How might you better implement boundaries using the One, Two, Three Clunk Theory?

• With whom is it appropriate to share information about your marriage and divorce? With whom should you avoid sharing your personal information?

Use the space below to move through your consideration of the above questions:

_____

_____

_____

_____

_____

_____

_____

_____

Chapter 10

Selecting Healthy Support

*"We all need care and support at sometime in
life, it does not matter how strong you are,
allow another to give love."*

– Leon Brown

Supportive friends and family are essential to a balanced and healthy life. We are designed to seek connection, and we struggle when in isolation. Social support is an important consideration in moving through a loving divorce. You will find comfort in having friends and/or family who support you emotionally and offer distraction with more pleasant activities and ideas when you are in distress. But it is also important to be selective in choosing who you lean on this time. While it may feel good to surround yourself with those who validate your negative feelings, like blame or anger, it is important to think about whether these people are in line with your post-divorce vision. Well-meaning friends and family can mirror our negative emotions in an attempt to provide empathy. Often, others reflect back to us our expressed negative emotions, like fear or anger, when they offer advice. Let's be honest, this feels really good in the moment! I mean, we all want to believe the way we see things is right. But in reality, this feedback can add unwanted fuel to the fire of our emotional upset and complicate our already difficult experience.

Take a moment to reflect on your social and familial circle and decide which individuals would provide healthy emotional, mental, or spiritual counsel. Think about with whom it might be better to refrain from seeking counsel. It is also worth mentioning here that the people we *wish* we could lean on (like parents) are not always the most ideal option and may leave us feeling more upset, rejected, or shamed. Take a moment to consider, *realistically*, who you may be tempted to include in your support circle, but will be more likely to deplete your resources than replenish them.

Lastly, let us consider the influence our social circles have on our behavior. You likely have an idea of the behaviors that will support the atmosphere of your post-divorce vision and which will instead cause pain or suffering. You might be thrilled to experience the freedom of separation and be eager to socialize, but if your intention is to refrain from drinking, drug use, or sexual encounters, you would do well to avoid scheduling social time with those who would entice you into these behaviors. Be honest with yourself about how you are impacted by your social and family relationships.

Chapter 10 Tools:

- Take a moment to decide who, in your life, would provide you with healthy support. You may want to consider which people in your life have greater emotional maturity, capacity for empathy, will leave you feeling supported or uplifted, and demonstrate an ability to keep your personal information private.

- Also consider those from whom you might *want* support, but will not be able to get it in a healthy manner. This would include those that will criticize or attempt to control your decisions based on their personal life experience and perspectives. No one can make your choices but you. Be cautious about allowing toxic people in as your support!

- Pause here to reflect if you are ready to commit to seeking support and sharing personal information only in the places that will support you? Can you agree to limit your choices to those that will serve your best interests (like refraining from self-destructive behavior)?

Use the space below to outline your plan for support:

_____

_____

_____

_____

_____

Chapter 11

Supporting Spiritual Connections

*"Where the soul is stirred, nurtured, and moved
by the sacred, there is spirituality."*

– Dr. David Elkins

Whether or not you are religious, you likely have some sort of spirituality if you have made it this far in this book. Whether this is a religious practice or engaging in artistic activities, I honor the vast spectrum of all things spiritual and encourage you to call upon any activities that allow you turn inward, leaving you feeling connected to something bigger than yourself. For some people, this is a perfect time to become involved in a religious group or get involved in activities within your current religious organization. For others, engaging in meditation or visualization—like the Lovingkindness meditation and other spiritual exercises throughout this book—will provide a sense of spiritual support. Still others may elect to revisit old artistic interests or take up new ones. All kinds of different endeavors can bring us in touch with something greater than ourselves and provide healthy distraction.

Dr. David Elkins (1998) writes, "The sacred is revealed through those experiences in life that touch the soul and fill us with a sense of poignancy, wonder, and awe." For those who do not identify with a more traditional concept of spirituality, I urge you to consider what activities you have engaged in that leave you in "the zone." It is my perspective that being in *flow* or *the zone* is its own kind of connection to something greater. Much like in a good meditation, the troubles of the world fall away, allowing you to tap in to the experience of simply *being*. This is not the same as distracting yourself with *busyness* like chores and work. Finding a path to the sacred can include any number of things—but it often involves art, music, silence, or nature. Perhaps you sing, play an instrument, paint, or build model airplanes. Is there a sport or other activity that leaves you feeling at peace, like you've hit reset when it's completed? Or perhaps, you feel lost in time, so entranced, it is as if the world has fallen away? What allows you to connect to something greater than yourself, touches your soul, or brings deeper meaning to your life? Now is the perfect time to prioritize these spiritual activities to help you connect with divine energy, your higher power, or your best self.

Chapter 11 Tools:

- Before moving into Section III, take a moment here to revisit your post-divorce vision. Notice if anything has changed and write it in the space below. Notice the feelings that arise as you imagine your vision and journal those feelings, if desired.

• Consider the possibilities of your vision and the positive impact this desired outcome could have on your future life (and your children's life, if applicable). Keep this idea in the back of your mind as you continue through Section III.

Use the space below to move through your consideration of the above ideas:

_____

_____

_____

_____

_____

_____

Section III

INTENTIONAL STEPS FOR
DIVORCING IN LOVE

With some mental and emotional wellness practice under your belt, it is time to consider the practical aspects of your divorce. The preparation from the previous chapters will support you as you move forward with interpersonal negotiations and legal decisions. While this difficult time may lead you to want to escape your discomfort and begin living life as a single person, I strongly encourage you to hold off on this and be conscientious of your choices. The chores of divorce are tedious and unpleasant. Gathering financial and legal documents, deciding on legal representation, determining living and custody arrangements are only a few of the tasks that await on the road to divorce. The chapters in this section are intended to offer preliminary insight into next steps as you move forward with your divorce. It is my hope that this will allow you to feel more prepared for the decisions that await and help you avoid some common divorce pitfalls.

As you move through the chapters that follow, check in with yourself periodically to effectively manage your emotional state. Remember that your emotions highlight what is important to you and you can use them to gain deeper insight. With regard to your divorce decisions, it is advised that you follow what you *feel* is right for you. There is no "right" answer for most things in life—though others might try to convince you otherwise. You cannot live your life trying only to please others...you will fail yourself every time.

"Some people believe holding on and hanging in there are signs of strength. However, there are times when it takes much more strength to know when to let go and then do it."

—Ann Landers

REBECCA HARVEY, PSY. D.

Chapter 12

Gaining Perspective:
Find Your Personal Pace

*"It is during our darkest moments that we
must focus to see the light."*
– Aristotle Onassis

The first step to a healthy divorce? **Slow down**. Slow down your mind, your emotional responses, and your physical reactions. Get perspective. Seriously, what's the rush?

We often operate under the misconception that there is somewhere else we need to be—and quickly. We believe if we hurry up we will feel "better" sooner. With something like ending a marriage, this is not exactly the case. Divorce is a grieving process that will happen in its own time. We cannot avoid our pain nor escape the disappointment that our marriage is ending. Even if we are content with a decision to terminate our nuptial agreement, most of us did not intend to divorce when we originally said, "I do." Because we had other ideas and dreams for our lives, there is some necessary grief and often confusion for most people that will occur, even beyond the divorce finalization.

As with our other emotions, there is much to be learned from the pain of our disappointment and grief. In my opinion, the greatest lesson to be learned is that the source of our problems—the cause of our suffering—is not our marriage *or* our divorce. It is our mind. Our ⸻ of things, the beliefs we hold tight, cause er ⸻ et. The time we spend thinking about emotionally upsetting issues creates our own suffering. Training your mind by learning to control your thoughts will reduce your suffering.

*our suffering
t our divorce.
is our mind.*

When emotions are stirred, as they often are in the ups and downs of a romantic relationship (and particularly during a divorce), we feel compelled to *react*—this is because we sense emotional "danger" and try to protect ourselves. As mentioned before, our brain doesn't know the difference between emotional pain and physical pain, so just as we might run from an actual bear to save our lives, we react with a similar response to emotional pain, and we mentally "run away" or fight to protect ourselves.

When our brain encounters a "problem," *sometimes* there is a real issue to be solved, but more often, we are mindlessly *reacting* or rather *overreacting* to our various feelings and thoughts, as we unproductively attempt to escape the perceived emotional "threat" of a situation. When this automatic response occurs at the wrong time, it deceptively leads us to reacting from a place of protection or attempting to solve an issue by thinking about it over and over. So, when our ex starts engaging in the behavior that pushes our buttons, our nervous system may respond as though there is a massive threat on the horizon. The issue that caused our emotion may be real. However, the illusion of the threat, and the reaction that we must find an immediate solution, or try make it "go away" with rumination is not. You may recall from earlier in the book that spinning or ruminating is a tremendous waste of time and energy and usually causes more emotional problems than it fixes. As Buddha taught, pain is necessary, but suffering is not. Suffering is avoidable through training our mind. Thus, the solution to reducing your suffering is not rushing through your divorce process to end your negative feelings, but working with your mind to quiet the part that says, "This is unbearable," or "I can't handle this." *Learning to differentiate the things you can change from the ones you would do better to accept is the key to a peaceful existence and a healthier mental life. Much like the serenity prayer, the goal is to grow in wisdom by working toward emotional maturity and focusing on the aspects of life that you can control.*

"God, grant me the serenity to accept the things I cannot change, the courage to change the things I can, and the wisdom to know the difference."

— Serenity Prayer

We begin to cultivate emotional maturity when we practice mindful self-awareness. As discussed earlier, mindful awareness allows us to be less reactive, slowing down and reflecting on a situation, including our thoughts and feelings, in that moment. From that mindful space, we can decide if the situation requires action to create a solution, or whether it is merely emotionally upsetting and can be responded to by being acknowledged, felt, and released. Deliberately slowing down your divorce, for example, allows you time to calm down and see things more clearly. Slowing your divorce process to a less intense pace can allow you to be present with your choices and less reactive. As a byproduct, you will most likely experience less regret surrounding your words and behaviors. When you can center yourself and keep your ultimate post-divorce vision in mind, you will behave more intentionally, as you let that vision guide your choices, despite the reactive impulses you may feel. Feeling the impulse is not the problem. Choosing to react from it is what gets you in trouble.

The tricky part is that by the time you reach the decision to divorce, there is often a sudden sense of urgency. You may have spent a considerable amount of time and energy reaching your decision and may now just want to get on with it. After all, *waiting* is an uncomfortable feeling for most, particularly when emotions are involved. While there are practical considerations, like finances and division of property to handle, rushing anything in life creates a much different experience than being present in the experience. I believe it is important when making decisions to remember, **you don't owe it to anyone to rush! And you owe it to yourself to be true to yourself.** During your consideration of divorce and your

> *Waiting is an uncomfortable feeling for most, particularly when emotions are involved.*

divorce process, allow this to be one boundary you uphold. I'm not suggesting you unnecessarily move at a snail's pace, but do not allow yourself to be rushed to a conclusion. Conversely, if you feel you are "dragging" the divorce out, perhaps from fear of being alone or out of anger toward your spouse, this is a good time to seek the help of a therapist so that you can process feelings and move your divorce along.

While an attorney can help you make informed decisions regarding pace and timing for certain legal processes, they cannot determine the emotional pace and timing that is right for you. Give yourself the mental space to move through your divorce at your own pace. Do not allow friends, family, your ex, or your attorney to control or manipulate your process. It is okay to say, "I will get back to you. I need a little more time to think." There may be instances where you cannot control the pace, as your partner is taking certain legal actions that require a timely response. If you are required to quicken your pace beyond what feels right, rely on the support skills you cultivated in Section II of this book and consider drawing upon the support of a therapist.

Despite pacifying our anxiety with the busyness of activity, rushing through important things often keeps us from making the decisions that will ultimately serve us best. Practically speaking, it may be wise to address certain pressing factors, for example, what your partner might do with shared finances or how you will share the news of separation with your children. Addressing practical issues such as these can reduce anxiety and allow you the time and mental space to process exactly how you want to move forward in your divorce. I have heard occasional stories in which one partner squandered money on a new love interest (ouch!), purchased extravagant personal items during a separation, or told the children about the separation or divorce independently, before the parents could tell the children together. So let's explore how you might address some realistic concerns while you simultaneously slow down your process.

To begin, let's explore some things that are more specifically a legal issue, like division of assets. In states where legal separation is recognized, it may prove beneficial to investigate this option. If you do not live in a state that allows legal separation, you may have an option to request a "Temporary Order" after you have filed a petition for divorce which can address child custody, financial support of children and/or spouse, and use of residence(s). The benefit of either of these options is that they can create a "time stamp" on the intent to separate and thus reduce some of the concern around income earned or money spent by each respective partner, as well as other practical concerns. This is one way to reduce your fear about how your estranged partner's emotionally-based decisions might impact you while you move through your decisions about divorce and toward reaching a settlement.

With a legal separation or other such temporary order in place, a judge would be able to more clearly observe the choices made by each partner after the time stamp or intent to separate has been expressed. Thus, if needed, the judge could take each partner's choices into consideration, if asset division is required as a legal decision. Choosing to place a legal time stamp on your separation puts "eyes" on each partner so that unkind behavior could be considered a violation of a legal agreement and result in being in contempt of court. Sharla Fuller, an attorney with Fuller Mediations in Dallas, suggests that a judge might be inclined, in the case of financial irresponsibility, to "redistribute funds more evenly by reconstituting as if the inappropriately spent funds were still a part of the total marital estate." In essence, the offending partner could receive fewer assets as a result of their spending. While you may not need to go this route, this is one consideration of how you can slow your divorce process while still protecting yourself and your assets. Most importantly, slowing down might create mental space to pay closer attention to other, arguably more important, aspects of divorce, like the climate you imagined in your post-divorce vision.

If you have already filed for divorce, one important factor in creating space is to consult with your attorney on the term or length of time allowed for the divorce. Fuller reports that in Texas some divorce courts will seek to dismiss your filing if the case remains pending for close to a year by sending you a notice and setting a hearing. Other courts may leave the divorce petition active in their system, allowing you considerably more time. It is important to discuss timing with your attorney, so you are advised in the most supportive way.

Divorce is not just about division of assets, custody agreements, and deciding who keeps the pets—which, for the record, are considered physical property, not custodial, like children. There are many emotions involved in the divorce process which have an impact on your physical, emotional, and spiritual health, and thus your general well-being. So let's explore some specific ways to slow down the divorce process and reduce the potential for unnecessary upset.

Chapter 12 Tools:

- Take some time to consider what pace is right for you. Are you rushing to "get your divorce done?" Do you agree with your partner's pace, or do you need a little more time to consider things, including your emotions? Are you possibly dragging the process on longer than necessary due to anger or fear? Use the space below to explore these questions.

- Remember that pain is unavoidable, but suffering is not necessary. Although our brains are wired for solving problems, we need to apply our mindfulness and some cognitive discipline to avoid ruminating, or spinning unnecessarily, on problems without solutions. Recall the serenity prayer!

_____

_____

_____

_____

_____

_____

Chapter 13

Consider Controlled Separation

"Living a love-based life requires creating intention and paying attention. Think before you proceed."

– Rebecca Harvey

Becoming more popular for couples considering divorce is a concept called "controlled separation." A Controlled Separation (CS) Agreement is an excellent option prior to or even after filing for divorce. Controlled separation serves as a non-legally binding agreement between separating partners navigating their separation process.

Choosing to engage in a controlled separation agreement can provide a couple with a "cooling-off period" to allow some distance from the emotional weight of their longstanding relationship issues. With this space, each person has an opportunity to take a look at their own contributions to the ineffective relational dynamics of the marriage. If you create a Controlled Separation Agreement with your partner, you can avoid some common transgressions that can further damage the relationship. The CS Agreement is negotiated between the couple with some guidance from a book or a therapist in an effort to determine in detail what will be allowed during the separation. Each partner has an opportunity to express what they want and need during the separation and what they are unwilling to offer. During this time, it is suggested that the couple come to an explicit agreement around the rules of engagement including living arrangements, amount and type of personal contact during separation, whether or not the couple will date others, and how and with whom they will share information about their separation. These agreements are designed to help reduce accidental (or intentional) hurt, which can complicate the separation experience and interfere with the possibility of reconciliation or achieving a healthy post-divorce relationship.

One hope with using a CS is that the couple will gain space and perspective on the state of their relationship and be able to move into a place of productive communication. With this accomplished, it is easier to determine the best course of action, as each person can respond intentionally rather than reactively. There are specific exercises and considerations throughout this book which will also assist you with perspective, emotional regulation, and communication. With some distance, you can often gain a clearer perspective of your partner, try out how it would feel to live apart from them, and allow them time to cool off. This might shift their manner of engaging. If this process does not serve to help repair and invigorate your marriage, it can assist with creating a better space to negotiate your differences and come to a mutual understanding around divorce settlement terms.

Lee Raffel, a therapist who worked extensively with couples, wrote a very useful book entitled *Should I Stay or*

Should I Go: A Guide to Controlled Separation. While there are other books addressing separation agreements, I have found this one to be wonderfully informative as it outlines the process by which couples can negotiate their terms of a trial separation. The twelve aspects of negotiation in Lee Raffel's (1997) CS contract include:

- **Time limits**: Separation for an agreed-upon time frame is established, typically one to six months.

- **Legal counsel**: Both partners agree not to file for divorce during the CS period.

- **Living arrangements:** The couple decides who will move out or the rules are set for an in-house separation.

- **Dividing home furnishings**: The couple divides home furnishings to ensure comfort and consider financial limitations.

- **Finances**: The couple determines a reasonable budget for separated living.

- **Children**: Children are prioritized and specific agreements around care and custody are arranged.

- **Couple's interpersonal relationship**: The couple agrees on the extent of continued interaction and intimacy. This includes phone calls, entering one another's residence, dealing with unexpected costs/repairs, family time together, holiday arrangements, and dating/sexual contact between one another.

- **Dating others**: The couple determines whether or not they will see others while separated.

- **Confidentiality**: The couple agrees about with whom they will discuss the separation.

- **Counseling**: The couple agrees to mediation or counseling to address non-negotiable aspects of the CS contract or to address relational issues.

- **Contract**: Changes can only be made to the contract if both parties discuss and agree in writing.

- **Termination of contract**: Both parties agree to notify verbally or in writing if they elect to terminate the contract prior to the agreed-upon time frame.

A controlled separation is often seen as a "last-ditch effort" to salvage a marriage by creating personal space for each partner. As you read these words, you may be quite certain there is no point in a trial separation period, as you could never get past the history of pain, discord, or the transgressions of your marriage. However, it has been my personal and professional experience that very often the hurts we once saw as insurmountable are forgivable (albeit not always understandable) with time and space. Best-case scenario, a Controlled Separation Agreement may afford you an opportunity to sort through the pain of the past and reach a place of forgiveness and renewed investment in your marriage. Worst-case scenario, you decide to divorce anyway, but possibly with more peace and confidence in your decision and increased clarity about yourself and your marriage.

If, even with time and space, the healthier choice for you and your partner is to end your marriage, Section IV will further explore how to best support your journey forward while managing your emotions and treating your estranged spouse with kindness and respect (even though you might not always want to do this). Even if you have not yet made your decision, you will likely find the remaining chapters of this section helpful in giving you increased knowledge of what is involved in the divorce process. In my experience, treating an ex with love, even in the midst of a painful separation or divorce, will leave you feeling better about yourself and your journey in your current relationship as well as in your next relationship.

Chapter 13 Tools:

• Consider implementing a Controlled Separation Agreement to establish terms of your pre-divorce marital separation—particularly if you are willing to consider reconciliation.

- Take a moment to consider what aspects of this agreement are most important to you and why?

_____

_____

_____

_____

_____

_____

_____

Chapter 14

Exploring Your Legal Options

*"The best way to solve problems and to fight
against war is through dialogue."*

– Malala Yousafzi

As most people are aware, hiring attorneys to battle out each party's side can be time-consuming, costly, and make the process often unnecessarily tumultuous. Keep in mind that attorneys make *more money* by spending *more time* working on your case. I am not suggesting that attorneys have malicious intent. In fact, I believe many attorneys are attempting to help inform you of your rights and "get you what you deserve." The problem here is that it is rarely as simple as it might initially sound and could result in long periods of litigation. An extensive attorney battle is not where I recommend "slowing down." In fact, this approach can become more of a "dragging out" of your divorce, in which there is a greater likelihood of emotional reactivity toward your partner. The greater likelihood is due to the stress of emotional ups and downs, inherent in divorce, alongside the necessary grieving process, converging with the exorbitant financial costs, and your constant attention to an upsetting process that feels like an unwanted second job. Not to mention, the more people involved in something, the more complicated communication can become.

Communication, when relayed indirectly and impersonally, creates far more opportunity for misunderstandings and unnecessary hurt. When other individuals (like two attorneys) are unnecessarily added to your divorce process, this is exactly the risk. Yet, in some cases, you may not have a choice, due to the behavior and choices of your partner. In these instances, you will need to do your best to maintain a kind and loving divorce attitude from within the parameters of the litigation process.

Survival in a Hostile Litigation: Olivia's Story

An example of this situation occurred for a client of mine who did not have an option for any form of mediation due to the hostile and aggressive stance of her partner, who wanted to "battle" her in court. This client, who I will call Olivia, arrived in my office seeking therapy in hopes of creating a positive home environment for her children and a greater experience of peace in her life following her tumultuous marriage.

Olivia left her difficult marriage after being physically assaulted by her husband. Though the assault was an isolated incident, the marriage had been in distress for years.

Affairs had taken place, and the couple often fought or did not address marital issues at all. Olivia was confident that the dissolution of the marriage was in the best interest of everyone, including their children.

A complicating factor for her was their tight-knit group of friends, some of whom had become entangled into the marriage dissolution and were now spreading gossip and intruding with questions and opinions regularly.

Olivia felt unsure about how to handle the energy from her estranged partner and the social intrusion she encountered in her daily life. My initial supportive therapy work included helping Olivia create boundaries and address communication with her ex and their social circle. Additionally, it was important for Olivia to address self-compassion for the state of her marriage and resulting divorce, establish self-care maintenance, and determine healthy outside support.

For Olivia, this involved clearing out unhealthy friendships, increasing time with supportive friends and family, engaging in fun activities with her children, focusing on communication with her children, and increasing exercise and other behaviors that served as a "reset" for her mentally. Lastly, using a court-monitored email application to communicate with her ex, attending church each week, and working through her emotions in weekly therapy sessions helped to support her emotional health.

Once Olivia found herself feeling more stable and less emotionally highjacked by her ex, she was able to examine relational dynamics in more depth, develop personal insight into her contributions to her difficulties, and thus began to view her marriage from a personal growth perspective. The skills she developed allowed her to continue to engage with her ex's ongoing difficult behavior in more productive and less upsetting ways, which now benefits her, her children, and any future relationship she may have.

When litigation is your only option, I strongly encourage you to select an attorney that can best represent *your values and needs* and allow you to set the pace that is right for you. In other words, *lead your attorney, do not be blindly led by your attorney.* Be particularly cautious of using your attorney as an emotional support as this can be costly—far more so than seeking therapy. Your attorney may respond to your fears, hurt, and anger with their best tools—further legal action. Keep in mind there's great potential for emotionally escalating your partner and inciting their legal representation to "retaliate" due to your own "posturing" or legal approach. If you make an aggressive move or respond in a way other than previously agreed upon with your ex, they will likely feel threatened and react accordingly. Furthermore, placing people between you and your partner can be like playing the telephone game, distorting communications as they are passed from person to person and losing the original intent by the time they reach the recipient—your partner. This is another reason to first attempt healthy and direct communication through controlled separation.

Chapter 14 Tools:

• Consider what your values and needs are in regard to your divorce and write down the top three to five below. Review your post-divorce vision before communicating with your partner about the divorce and prior to selecting an attorney. If you need to hire an attorney, find someone who is aligned with your vision.

_____

_____

_____

_____

_____

_____

_____

_____

Chapter 15

Putting Down the Gloves

"Our power lies in remaining nonreactive."

– Marianne Williamson

As I shared before, by the time I had elected to end my marriage, I was emotionally drained from trying to save it and was done fighting. My goal was to close out my marriage in a respectful and kind manner. I did not want to continue unproductive arguments and unnecessary emotional discomfort. It was for this reason I preferred to mediate rather than battle my ex in court. Yet, as a psychologist with no corporate-world experience who was divorcing a man who successfully negotiated with large international companies for a living, I often felt ill-equipped to navigate my own settlement. I feared I would need to hire a litigation attorney to know my rights, and that this would begin a battle I did not have the emotional or financial resources to handle. But, because of my desire to lead from a place of love, to be a Heart Warrior, I chose instead to manage my fearful thoughts and stay committed to a peaceful divorce process. My commitment guided my choice of legal representation (selected due to her alignment with my post-divorce vision goals) and led me to write this book.

If you intend to divorce in love, you need to be aware that there are multiple alternatives to "litigation," or the typical divorce battle. In traditional litigation, two attorneys are hired to "hash it out" for their clients. The alternative options I will discuss below allow divorcing spouses to decide between themselves what is best for each of them and, for those with children, what is in the best interest of their children. To better understand the difference between these options, I met with Dallas-based attorney, Sharla Fuller of Fuller Mediations. Fuller, a warm, compassionate, and intelligent woman, explained why she transitioned into mediation from litigation. "I was making people mad," she said, "even if I won in the litigation process. I was exacerbating conflict even though I was trying to help." When asked why mediation was preferred to litigation in general, she stated, "Mediation is a less awful way to do divorce. Not a better way, because it is still an awful time. But a good counselor, mediator, or facilitator can help people work things out."

> "Mediation is a less awful way to do divorce. Not a better way, because it is still an awful time. But a good counselor, mediator, or facilitator can help people work things out."
> ~Sharla Fuller

As Fuller's sentiment reflects, divorce is difficult, often confusing, potentially complicated, and always heart-breaking on some level. If you are someone in touch with your desire for emotional well-being—you are committed to cultivating peace, love, and equanimity (emotional balance), you must decide to put down the gloves and refrain from "fighting for fighting's sake." That is to say, you must allow your deeper internal commitment to your post-divorce vision to move you through this difficult experience. Expect that it will be hard. Expect that you will feel reactive in tense moments. But hold faith in your post-divorce vision, and make decisions in line with your best long-term goals. Below are some alternative considerations to the traditional divorce litigation approach.

Therapeutic Invitation:

As you read the mediation options that follow, listen to your inner voice, or "gut," and notice your physical and emotional state. If you're able to do so, name the emotion you experience and identify where you feel it in your body. It may help to write down your emotional response to each suggested option in the space provided below. Notice if this increased emotional awareness can assist you in deciding which option will best serve you.

_____

_____

_____

_____

_____

_____

_____

_____

<u>Cooperative Divorce</u>

One alternative to litigation is referred to as "cooperative divorce." In a cooperative divorce process, the couple can involve attorneys or reach an agreement between themselves on the broad and specific terms of their divorce. Things like division of real estate, liquid assets, liabilities, retirement funds, medical benefits, investments, retirement accounts, taxes, and legal fees from the divorce will be decided between the separating partners. Additionally, custody arrangements and child-related expenses will be agreed on by the couple. If the couple works out these agreements on their own, without assistance from an attorney, then one of the partners will take these conclusions to a mediation attorney who is hired by only one of the divorcing spouses, but will be able to prepare the legal paperwork as agreed upon by both parties. On reaching a successful agreement, the non-represented divorcing spouse will take the completed divorce agreement to a second attorney. That attorney will simply review the details and confirm that the terms of agreement meet the understanding of that spouse and request any necessary revisions.

In this model, there may be some final agreements settled between attorneys, if the partners are unable to agree. Therefore, it will be particularly helpful if you select your attorney based on your intention for a friendly and amicable divorce, as they will then be more committed to avoiding the legal battlefield. This is an ideal and substantially more affordable option for divorcing couples who are able to manage their emotional states long enough to be civil in their communication with each other. But, for those who are not able to be civil, choosing a cooperative divorce model could actually complicate and lengthen the divorce process. As Fuller noted, half-jokingly, "If one attorney (symbolically) throws a rock, the other attorney will often pick it up and throw it back." So, if you and your partner are unable to remain civil, and a battle seems unavoidable, one of the next two options below may be a more suitable approach.

Collaborative Coaching

A second option is to hire a mediation therapist, coach counselor, or cooperative parenting facilitator, who (unless court-mandated) serves as a neutral entity. Since they are not hired or assigned by your legal representation, they operate separately from the court system and your attorneys. These coaches offer sessions in which the couple will improve necessary communication skills. This is important because communication may have broken down during the marriage and often will have contributed to the decision for divorce. A mediator is not representing either divorcing partner and therefore does not give legal advice to either person. They instead must remain in a neutral position, focused only on facilitating purposeful communication between the parties. The increased communication skills are intended to assist the couple in setting the terms of the divorce agreement (usually completed during the sessions). This can facilitate healthy communication in general, which will be particularly helpful if you have children to co-parent in an ongoing capacity. Keep in mind that for those with children, you are not only in each other's lives until your child is a legal adult, but will often see one another at graduations, holidays, birthdays, and other important life events for decades to come (or even the rest of your life).

Use of a collaborative coach in mediation usually speeds up the agreement of terms, which facilitates the divorce process by creating a foundation of understanding for both parties (something that can get lost when having attorneys battle the terms on your behalf). This arrangement can be paced by the couple, which works well for those who need to take a little extra time and space to better manage their emotional responses or come to decisions with less emotional upheaval.

An additional benefit of this option is that if you hire a child therapist or child advocate as your facilitator, they can more directly consider your child's needs. This can create a clearer picture of what is in the best interest of your child and identify important areas of communication and growth to support your efforts to co-parent your child.

Active Mediation

In a third option, the couple schedules an appointment with a neutral party mediator to actively mediate, in the moment. Each party may or may not have their individual attorney representation present, depending on what option they have selected. In this role, a mediator's job is to facilitate communication and negotiations (just like in the cooperative divorce model), while suggesting creative compromises, keeping the couple on track, and encouraging empathy in the midst of what is usually an emotionally charged experience. A mediator can reduce the occurrence of reactive behaviors, like arguments, name-calling, and side-tracking to unresolved issues of the past. Although this may differ state to state, in Texas, a mediator cannot offer legal advice to either divorce partner and must remain neutral in a mutually beneficial perspective for both parties.

Sharla Fuller explained that mediation can occur in several ways. To give an inside view of an active mediation process, I will use Sharla's personal approach to exemplify. Her first step is to have clients complete a questionnaire regarding their goals and their understanding of their partner's goals, prior to mediation. She believes this helps get their mindset into a healthier and more cooperative place for negotiation of terms during mediation. In her practice, Fuller personalizes her approach to the needs of her clients. Appointments are typically scheduled as full- or half-day events, though, when conducting mediation without attorneys, she reported that the process typically occurs over multiple days with shorter (two-hour) periods. At the close of each day, each person is given "homework" to complete prior to the next appointment. These shorter mediation sessions, without attorneys, usually occur with the couple in the same room. She reported that the time frame for these shorter mediation sessions is largely determined by the amount of assets, number of child-related decisions to be made, and how quickly both partners can process information and reach their final decisions. This option worked well for my own divorce. Our assets were not complicated, and we were able to discuss division of assets in a calm and respectful manner. In fact, this step of our process felt surprisingly simple.

The more typical case Fuller mediates is one in which each party is in a separate room with their own attorney, as the mediating attorney/mediator goes between the rooms facilitating the terms of divorce or other family law issues. Naturally, if one or both parties refuses to budge on an issue, resorts to fighting, or refuses to communicate, this can lengthen or sabotage the mediation efforts, resulting in the need for a more typical attorney-driven divorce process. Unfortunately, I have heard of this happening for my own clients all too often. When emotions run high, some individuals seem to hold tight to their desire to fight. The spouse who is ready to comes to terms reports an experience of confusion around behavior that appears "illogical," especially when the settlement being offered is split in the favor of the resistant partner. Interestingly, Fuller reports that her firm often receives cases in which the opposite is occurs. In other words, she finds that after extended and exhausting fights, many couples decide to switch to a mediation approach to expedite the process, reduce additional expenditure, and spare further emotional anguish.

She reported that most of her clients are three to six months into the divorce process, when the parties "decide not to waste more time or money fighting; they're tired, so they switch to mediation." She compared the cases in which people ultimately switch from litigation to mediation to having a car stuck in the mud. "People are more invested the deeper they are in the litigation process.

They feel like they can't settle because of all the time and money they have already invested. Like a car stuck in the mud, the tires just keep spinning, but they're not getting anywhere, and the ruts just get deeper. It's hard to break that pattern." She added, "It's best for people if we can get them in before they have gone through all that heartache and loss of time and money." If you have already begun your divorce process in a traditional litigation model, take a moment to consider if switching to mediation could spare you additional financial and emotional pain.

While other mediation firms may be slightly different in their style, the general approach is likely similar. Mediating attorneys can help you have a less dramatic or traumatizing divorce experience. As suggested earlier, take another moment to consider your post-divorce vision and how each of the three suggested options feels as you try them on. Which one feels more realistic for you to consider or work toward? Without deciding for your partner, decide which option is best for *you* as your preferred approach to divorce. Remember, divorce is emotionally difficult regardless of the option you choose. Do not expect it to be simple. Align your expectations to allow yourself the time and space to handle this difficult process in the best manner possible.

Your various divorce fall across a spectrum, with litigation as "full-out nuclear war" on one end and cooperative agreements on the other. As Fuller explained, "If a couple sits down at the kitchen table and comes to terms on their own and then has attorneys write it up and negotiate, that's the simplest way." Mediation, the main focus of Fuller Mediations, is less expensive than litigation, but can still be costly, depending on the couple's needs. However, she noted that mediation can be the best option for parents who need help working out their settlement terms, or couples who become highly emotional with one another and are unable to reach an agreement between themselves. It is also an ideal option for those wishing to limit public exposure to matters of their private life and to reduce costly attorney fees and court visits.

In your practical consideration of litigation over mediation, it is important to review a few key points. Online estimates suggest that a court-battled divorce can take six times as long as mediation (averaging 18 versus 3 months) and be five times as costly (averaging $15,000 versus $3,000). In the case of Fuller Mediations, which handles both low- and high-profile cases, the high-profile litigation can cost "anywhere up into the millions," as compared to mediation, costing typically $500–$5,000. Regardless of your financial picture, the respective financial savings of the mediation option is undeniable. Not to mention the difference between the emotional experience of reaching an agreeable compromise as opposed to enduring an anger-infused litigation battle. Often, after a lengthy and expensive battle, both parties may walk away feeling they lost, and both will be emotionally exhausted. Further, all court records around a divorce can be public domain, and strangers are allowed to be present in the court room, which compromises your privacy. On the other hand, mediation is a confidential, private, and controlled experience focused on the best interests of the divorcing couple and their children, without well-meaning attorneys inadvertently creating roadblocks.

Chapter 15 Tools:

- Is it possible for you to consider bypassing a more traditional litigation divorce, which often lends itself to "fighting," and instead consider an alternative approach?

- If so, consider and write down which option from above feels best to you. Take a moment to consider how you might approach your estranged partner to share these alternatives and attempt to come to an agreement that might work for both of you. What would be the best time and manner in which to approach the conversation with your ex? You might consider requesting an allotted amount of time on a specific day to have this conversation. (For example, "Can you set aside 20–30 minutes this Friday evening to discuss something I have been considering?")

_____

_____

_____

_____

_____

_____

Chapter 16

Hiring Your Attorney

*"You are always just one decision away from a
completely different life. Choose wisely."*

– Rebecca Harvey

If you do elect to file for divorce, you may need to hire an attorney. As mentioned previously, I strongly encourage you to find one that is willing and able to keep *your* goals at the center of their focus. I have often witnessed individuals selecting their attorney based on the attorney's reputation for being intimidating, ruthless, or "winning" a high settlement for their clients. That decision has been explained to me as a stance to intimidate their partner or manage their own fear of the divorce process. Keep in mind that this approach can set a negative or aggressive tone for the divorce. It can serve to create fear and defensive posturing in your ex, which may result in them finding an equally intimidating attorney or behaving with a more aggressive approach in the divorce process. This strategy all too often results in wasted time, money, and unnecessary emotional pain, and I advise you to consider it only as a last resort.

Sometimes when divorcing, it is the case that people become so focused on "winning," they miss the emotional damage being created in the battle. Fuller stressed the importance of attorneys seeing their clients' "big picture," as clients often are blinded by emotions. If you make it a priority, it is possible to find an attorney who will be an ally in your post-divorce vision. If you fail to do so, you may find yourself in a Pyrrhic victory, in which you win the war, but the devastating toll of that "win" leaves you feeling ultimately defeated.

It is crucial that your attorney is able to remain objective in working toward your desired outcomes, rather than being pulled into your emotional process as they represent you. Because of this, it is important that you not vent to your attorney. Both attorney Sharla Fuller and Child Advocate Dr. Julie Carbery offered this same advice. Many people vent to their legal representative, and it becomes the most expensive and ineffective therapy possible. Keep in mind, your attorney is not trained to emotionally advise you and typically bills by the hour. Furthermore, losing sight of this boundary can further complicate the process of your divorce. Fuller stated, "I can't tell you whether you want a divorce. I can't effectively help you make that decision; that's what counseling is for." Her suggestion was to take time to decide if divorce is right for you, and in most cases, it is best to "wait to file [for divorce] until you are certain...as lawyers are not in the best position to guide your decision."

It is Fuller's suggestion that individuals *thoroughly research* their attorney before hiring one to be certain that the attorney's approach is in line with their goals and personal style. If it is your intention to have the kindest and most peaceful divorce process possible, she stressed the importance of being able to manage your attorney's aggression, rather than allowing them to control the whole process for you. She specifically refers to the fact that it is you who may have an ongoing relationship with your ex-partner; your attorney will not. It is important for you to remember that your attorney is invested in your divorce process in a different way than you are. They cannot be as interested in your future life and ongoing relationships. Therefore, it is essential you avoid any aggressive legal behavior which could ignite unwanted chaos and drama and result in negative long-term effects on your relationship.

Therapeutic Invitation:

Keeping your ultimate goal in mind during this process, ponder the following questions: If you have children, do you want to have a peaceful co-parenting relationship following your divorce? Do you want to perpetuate an ongoing pattern of anger and aggressive acting-out toward the person you once loved? Do you want to keep the energy of your divorce calm for the sake of your own and your children's health? Would you rather your money be spent on hefty divorce costs or be saved for your (or your children's) future?

The choice is ultimately yours. Of course, you cannot control what your partner may do, but *if your goal is divorcing in love, it is important to focus on your vision,* rather than being reactively caught up in fear and anger.

Chapter 16 Tools:

• After considering the therapeutic suggestion above, you should feel some clarity about your goals regarding the divorce process and outcome. Remember to keep these at the center of your focus as you select your attorney.

• Research attorneys, rather than jumping at the first one you come across. Be sure you are hiring an attorney who can keep you goals in mind and help manage legal interactions in a respectful manner to reduce unnecessary emotional and mental strife.

*If you do not have children, you may want to skip ahead to Chapter 18.

Chapter 17

Consider a Co-Parenting Facilitator

*"It is easier to build strong children than to
repair broken men [and women]."*

– Frederick Douglass

If there are children involved in your divorce process, it is imperative that you consider how your current behavior will directly impact them now, as well as in the future. **The tone you and your partner create and maintain *right now* makes all the difference.** This is not easy terrain to navigate. Divorce is laden with an array of confusing and negative emotions. However, there are many specialized professionals that can facilitate healthy communication and consideration of your child's individual needs as you decide your settlement terms and move through divorce, including realistic expectations of child support and ongoing custody agreements. *Becoming quality co-parents is, in my opinion, the most important factor in your marital dissolution.* If you are not in a position logistically or financially to consider even a few sessions of specialized therapy for your child and co-parenting needs, you may consider reading more on the subject, like *The Coparents' Communication Handbook: Answers to Your Top Twenty Questions,* by Susan Boyan and Ann Marie Termini. Using their co-parenting and divorce workbook is also a good way to keep your child at

REBECCA HARVEY, PSY. D.

the center of your decisions. These types of resources, in addition to professional assistance, can make all the difference in a non-contentious or family-friendly divorce process.

Many couples believe their children are oblivious to the struggles in their marriage and unaware of any hostility between the parents. Dr. Julie Carbery,

> *Even very young children are aware, but afraid to address...*

a highly experienced child-centered Co-Parenting Facilitator and Child Advocate, strongly disagrees. According to Dr. Carbery, "Even very young children are aware, but afraid to address [what they see occurring between their parents] for fear of their world crumbling." In fact, Dr. Carbery has witnessed children communicating "the heaviness of the emotional undercurrent as young as two-and-a-half years old." Many times, this leads to the child shutting down or acting out.

If your child is acting out in the midst of your divorce process, it is especially crucial to seek professional support from a child advocate or co-parenting specialist. Many people are not familiar with a child advocate or co-parenting facilitator, which is "very different from a child therapist," Dr. Carbery explains. A child advocate is a child therapist with specialized training in divorce, mediation, and co-parenting facilitation. This person is focused on keeping the child's best interest at heart in all decisions. Dr. Carbery trained with Susan Boyan and Ann Marie

Termini, the originators of the co-parenting facilitation concept and has long been considered an expert in her field. Though many parents come to her early in their divorce process, courts often mandate this type of therapeutic support to protect the child's best interests. In fact, it is most often court-mandated in cases where divorcing partners are unable to get along or the child's welfare is in question.

In explaining the difference between these child-focused professionals, Dr. Carbery divided facilitating consultants into two camps. A co-parenting facilitator is someone who can help you mediate the terms of your custody agreement in a more amicable manner. This is opposed to having attorneys battle the terms, which can create further turmoil for everyone involved—including the children. A child advocate, such as Dr. Carbery, is primarily focused on training both parents to become more child-centered in their approach. She reported that in her experience, "Often, one parent is naturally more child-centered." However, when co-parents meet with her, they can get help creating a negotiated solution to their parenting questions. For instance, if one parent believes the child is ready to start driving at age sixteen and the other parent disagrees, a joint solution in the child's best interest and safety is developed and agreed upon by both parents. It is her job to listen between the lines, observe dynamics, and keep them focused on the present moment and best interest of their child, rather than diverting into old arguments around past transgressions and unresolved personal matters. As such, she establishes rules of engagement that center around the child's specific needs. It is often the case that Dr. Carbery consults with other co-parenting facilitators, attorneys, or divorce mediators that may be involved in the process while she serves as a child-focused advocate. This allows her a more comprehensive perspective on family dynamics and gives her an idea of how to best represent and support the child's needs. Further, when the situation allows, she consults with the couple's attorneys to better understand the family dynamics and assist comprehensively. Frequently, in cases where couples require litigation around custody and other child-related decisions, Dr. Carbery is called to testify in court hearings about the overall well-being of the child. At this time, she speaks to the court about the parental dynamics she has observed and their impact on the child, including both parents' adherence to the agreed-upon rules. This becomes an accountability measure that is built into the divorce process in hopes of keeping both parents on their best behavior. Thus, if you are genuinely concerned about your ex's parenting, including parenting-related lifestyle choices or their capacity to care for the children in a safe and healthy manner, having a child advocate adds additional transparency and thus reassurance that your child's needs will be represented and considered.

When asked about the importance of child advocacy during divorce, Dr. Carbery stated that often even very good parents are so emotionally entangled in their own grief and transition that they are exhausted and cannot handle the additional needs of the child's grief and their adjustment to the transition. Seeking therapeutic intervention at this time "ensures the child is getting *some* of their needs met," she reasons. She suggested therapy as one way to assist a child in making sense of this confusing time in which they may be empathizing with one parent over another. This can occur even if the parents attempt not to pull their children into their conflict, as children may perceive one parent as "winning" and another as "losing." She warned that occasionally, children lose the ability to function normally in school, sports activities, social life, and activities of daily living as they are emotionally preoccupied. What occurs at this time is a primitive biological function. Their prefrontal cortex is interrupted in its function due to the heightened state of anxiety and their threat to life as they know it. Without our prefrontal cortex "online," we are less able to perform higher level thinking and attend to stimuli like school lessons or requests to complete chores. This neurobiological phenomenon is often referred to as "fight or flight" mode and is the same place a parent might find themselves when navigating the terrain of divorce.

Similar to their divorcing parents, children wonder, "How is divorce going to change my world?" And more frightening still, "Who is going to take care of me?" Carbery witnesses that often the child reports that *they* are going through a divorce. Things can become especially complicated for a child when there is a third party involved (new partner, affair, etc.). Sometimes, the child blames the third party and is unable to fully comprehend the complex nature of divorce. Involving a child advocate/facilitator and/or co-parenting facilitator is a way to reduce damage by ensuring that a professional can assist your child in processing their feelings and understanding things in a developmentally appropriate manner. Whether the child is two-and-a-half or seventeen, they need to process their emotions properly to maintain healthy brain function and a healthy lifestyle.

In assuring your child is healthy during this time, "the most important consideration," according to Dr. Carbery, is to "give children a voice." She asserted that those children who feel they have an outlet, "even if only for a couple of sessions," seemed to adjust better in later developmental stages of acceptance about the divorce process (i.e., house sale, parents dating, blending families, etc.). "Children who are told it has nothing to do with them and are not given a voice suffer in long-term development, identity, and acceptance of their future new family structure."

Children understand marital relationships and the termination of relationship differently at different stages of their emotional development. Having a child specialist involved can assist in meeting their needs at their own current developmental level. They can also offer insight about whether the child might benefit from follow-up therapy at a later developmental stage, when they are attempting to process old information with a new capacity of understanding. For example, Dr. Carbery noted that young children have difficulty grasping abstract concepts and needed things explained in a concrete and practical manner, whereas a teen may need assistance understanding healthy romantic relationship dynamics and conflict management even years after their parents' divorce. Furthermore, some children will need to reprocess their childlike understanding of the divorce when they reach college age and are transitioning to adulthood.

When asked to share thoughts on basic areas of awareness for parents with children going through the divorce process, Dr. Carbery said, "Everyone wants a whole, intact family unit; it provides a secure base. When this is threatened, children begin grasping for security and stability in various forms—some less than ideal." She added that most kids wish their parents would reconcile, even many years post-divorce, even if logically it is unrealistic. When children reference their parents' divorce by saying, "It's for the best," she believes they are attempting to be logical to avoid their emotions or to take care of their parents' emotions. Take a moment to consider all of the behaviors adults partake in, often without realizing they are doing so, to "soothe" or "escape" difficult emotions. Even if we set aside the more dramatic, illegal, or risky behaviors, it is socially normed for adults to engage in many unhealthy coping behaviors in excess. This includes drinking alcohol (or in some states, smoking marijuana), shopping, gambling, or having sex, etc. Each of these behaviors gives us an immediate high, or release of chemicals that leaves us (temporarily) feeling better. Now consider what is available to your children to soothe themselves on their own. Their resources are significantly more limited. It is up to you, as the parent, to help them find healthy ways to cope. For this reason, keeping your children's well-being as the center focus, as best you can, during your divorce is strongly encouraged. There are many ways to facilitate your child's welfare that require only minimal effort.

In regard to basic rules of engagement during separation and divorce, Dr. Carbery firmly believes you should never speak poorly of your ex-partner in front of your children. "Anything you say negatively to or about your co-parent in front of your child, you may as well be saying to and about your child, as this i_ .._ .. .._. ..'ill internalize it. Remember, your children are a *part* of you and your co-parent." Carbery warns, "Kids listen when you don't think they are, and they will read your email, texts, etc.," and sometimes never let you know. To this point, simply texting horrible things to someone about your partner may be discovered by your child and be detrimental to their mental and emotional wellbeing. If you are not referring to your ex by their first name, Dr.

Carbery encourages parents to refer to one another as "my co-parent" rather than "my ex" or some other commonly used references that can be perceived as negative, to keep things in a positive and appropriate framework for your children. Another rule is not sharing detailed information about costs, court events, custody terms, personal grievances, emotional struggles, and possible life changes that are not imminent (like consideration of moving homes or cities/schools). Part of a loving divorce process is keeping things as peaceful and stable for your children as possible. All of this impacts your family's emotional climate now and for years or even decades to come.

Regardless of your decision to remain in the marriage or dissolve it, co-parents are encouraged by Dr. Carbery to cooperatively create a unique "parenting plan" that meets the needs of the child. Parenting plans can even be used as a temporary solution with a shorter timeline that addresses how certain immediate needs will be handled. For instance, parents might agree at the start of separation to try a fifty/fifty custody agreement and outline a plan to be signed by both parents. One example could be: "For the next six weeks, the child will spend a week at a time with each parent in order to achieve a fifty-fifty custody arrangement and determine if there are any aspects that do not serve the child's best interest." After a six-week period, co-parents are asked to consider such factors as:

1. Does the child seem happy and content in both homes?

2. Is the child sleeping well at both homes?

3. Is the child arriving to school and being picked up in a timely manner, no matter which home they sleep at that week?

Reviewing these factors with the best interest of the child in mind can allow time to troubleshoot any problems that arise. Ultimately, using a personalized plan of this nature will allow parents to come to a more objective (and tested) decision of what will work best for their child. This can assist in reaching an agreement on matters of custody within the divorce decree. A sample agreement can be found at the close of this chapter. Keep in mind this can be modified for each child and each matter of concern and can be adjusted as needed and signed by each parent. Further, if you are unable to come to amicable terms on your own, you are encouraged to seek services with a co-parent facilitator.

Parenting Tip

There are many ways to remain child-focused while disengaged as parents. Regularly communicating about the child, with a third-party present, can be beneficial, assuming both parties agree to refrain from criticism and fighting. A professional is the best third-party option to use in these situations.

Parents can also keep a journal about their child that discusses things like their mood, eating habits, and sleep behavior as well as other activities reported at school or seen at home that would be relevant to share. Having this type of non-direct communication can serve to ease the child's transition between homes. In Parallel Parenting, the best plan is to communicate electronically, so there is a record of interaction. In situations in which one or both parents are not communicating in a healthy manner, there are software applications, such as My Family Wizard, that retain e-communication between parents and makes it accessible to the judge, as needed. This visibility is intended to reduce hostile interactions and encourage parents to engage in respectful behavior.

> ### *Parenting Tip*
>
> *Some parents will not be able to co-parent due to intense conflict. Keep in mind that some of these dynamics might still allow for "Parallel Parenting." This style of parenting is an arrangement that occurs when parents remain disengaged from one another, but agree to prioritize the child and their individual relationship with the child. This can sometimes be used as a platform to later move into co-parenting after the emotional dust has settled and trust has been established by both parents cooperating respectfully.*

Chapter 17 Tools:

- Take some time to consider your children. Not from a perspective of the grief or guilt you may feel about your decision to divorce, but rather from a place of empathy and consideration of what they need. What might serve them best in regards to a co-parenting dynamic? How can you contribute to creating this dynamic?

- How is your child doing? Are they acting out in school? Do they not seem themselves? Have you noticed any mood shifts or aggressive behavior? If so, consider seeking professional guidance to help them adjust. Keep in mind that even if your child is not exhibiting obvious signs, they would likely benefit from discussing the divorce with someone.

- Remember to speak kindly about your ex, or not at all. Even when you do not think your children are listening, they may be. If they are in the vicinity, refrain from speaking negatively. Refer to your co-parent by their first name or "my co-parent." Whatever negative statement you are making about your ex, your child may be internalizing as being about them.

- Consider what areas of your child's life would benefit from a parenting plan and use the sample provided on the next page to create your own (sample provided by Dr. Julie Carbery).

Use the space provided below to answer the above questions about your children's needs:

_____

_____

_____

_____

_____

_____

_____

_____

Co-Parenting Worksheet Sample

Co-parenting Agreements for a successful summer and transition to new school for (CHILD'S NAME).

1. Parents will engage in a physical activity with __(CHILD)__ for 45 minutes per day (list specific activities).

2. Parents will keep __(CHILD)__ on a routine schedule all summer in preparation for transition to new school and encourage general emotional regulation. Summer schedule wake-up and bedtime will be 6:30-8:30 with an hour extension to either time this summer. That is, __(CHILD)__ can be awakened between 6:00-7:00 each morning and go to bed between 8:00-9:00 each night.

3. Parents will have __(CHILD)__ do an instant replay (do over) around any negative self-talk.

4. Parents will agree to install software that regulates how much screen time __(CHILD)__ gets each day and agree on reasonable limits to set.

5. Parents will attempt to arrange an outing or playdate with __(CHILD'S)__ classmates at new school this summer.

_____   _____
Parent signature   Parent signature

_____   _____
Date   Date

Chapter 18

Communicating for Negotiation

"The single biggest problem in communication is the illusion that it has taken place."

– George Bernard Shaw

Communication is the biggest behavioral factor in healthy relational outcomes. In fact, couples' therapists spend a considerable amount of time helping couples learn to truly *listen* to one another, as opposed to *assuming* they understood the message, which leads to unnecessary discord. Communication is another area where slowing down your process is beneficial. As you read on, you will find considerations for communicating as clearly as possible, refraining from assumptions, avoiding passive-aggressive communication, hostile words, and tone. As a healthy reminder, when your best efforts are failing you, *take time out and revisit the discussion at a later time.*

"Most people do not listen with the intent to understand; they listen with the intent to reply."

– Stephen R. Covey

Listen to Your Partner

Regardless of the style of divorce process you choose, communication is the most critical element. If you are able to communicate in a healthy manner, you might be surprised at what you can accomplish. Keep in mind, you do not have to get your partner to communicate in a healthy way to maintain *your* commitment to a heathy style of engaging. "Taking the high road" is not always easy, but you will ultimately feel better when you do.

Listening goes a long way. Despite how often I see couples take the stance of arguing to be "right," the truth is what we all really want is to be *heard.* It is amazing how someone's emotions de-escalate when they feel heard. The best way to accomplish this is with empathic listening. Empathic listening involves being able to paraphrase what you heard the speaker say, validate what they have said, and express some level of empathy. Validation does not mean you agree with them. As a therapist, I don't always agree with people's perspectives or their choices. But I can certainly find a way to validate their perspective as reasonable for a person with their life experience and current views of the world. When we engage in dialogue this way, we hopefully leave others feeling heard, which can help to regulate their emotions and increase the likelihood that they will be willing to hear our position as well.

What this might look like is your ex-partner telling you they are mad that you didn't complete a task as they would have liked. Rather than defending yourself as to why you didn't do something a certain way or why you believe their perspective is wrong (both common stances), you *listen* to their complaint and find *some bit of reality in it.* This might mean telling them you hear they are upset—the message is received—and you can see how they came to believe you would complete it a certain way—validating their reality, whether or not you actually share the same reality. Finally, express that given their perspective, you can understand why they would be upset. It's that simple. Nowhere in the exchange must you admit you are in the wrong, nor that they are in the right. From this point, you can go on to discuss how to resolve the situation. This type of healthy conflict resolution cannot be put into practice if parents are stuck defending their opposing stances.

The secret to empathic listening is that you must make a genuine effort and not use the technique in a passive-aggressive manner. Delivering any part of the communication with contempt, sarcasm, or an aggressive, angry, or condescending tone will further anger your ex—understandably so. However, if you make a genuine effort to hear what they are saying, you might find yourself moving through necessary conversations more quickly, facilitating your separation and divorce process and supporting your post-divorce vision.

Create Space When Needed

Sometimes, even if one partner is engaging in empathic listening, the conversation will become heated or aggressive in nature. Nothing productive happens when this occurs. The best you can hope for when aggression enters the scene is that one partner will back down and give in to end the conflict at hand. This "resolution," if we can call it that, may or may not last due to the manipulative duress under which it was obtained. It is far less productive to negotiate when negative emotions are activated.

When you find yourself emotionally "worked up," the best thing you can do is take a "time out." Time out is just as it sounds. It's no different than a sports team taking a break to gather themselves and plan their best strategy, or removing your toddler from the current environment in a moment when they are upset. Taking a time out allows us to calm our nervous system so that we can re-engage our frontal lobe (which, if you recall, is necessary for higher-level thinking as well as planning and executing consciously-chosen behavior).

The obstacle with regard to time outs is that in the moment you need it, you will rarely want to take it. When our primitive brain is triggered and the fight or flight response kicks in, the last thing we want to do is stop. We are revved up and ready for action. Our nervous system is in a sympathetic response state and cueing our mind and body

190

for action. In order to increase the likelihood of taking a time out, you must plan ahead that this is what you will do in a moment of high stress or emotional activation and mindfully pay attention to your body cues, in order to catch yourself before you react. It is not necessary, but if you can get your partner to agree to this strategy in advance, it will be easier for you to implement in the moment. Keep in mind that even if you have already crossed the line and said hurtful or unproductive things, it is still a good idea to call a time out to prevent further damage from being inflicted.

Refrain from Hostility and Battles

Sometimes, while ending a marriage and experiencing the host of negative emotions that come along with the process, it feels good to release your negative emotions...on your estranged partner. And while it may feel good to verbally "beat up" your partner, it will not serve your best interest. Using the time out technique, self-soothing behavior, and a commitment to refraining from hostile interactions are the best ways to keep interactions as productive as possible. To release the negative emotions you harbor, you may consider journaling, exercising (for example, boxing classes are a great method to release built up emotional energy), talking with a close confidant, or seeking therapy. While it is important to move through your feelings, it is equally as important not to complicate your divorce by attacking your partner when your difficult feelings arise.

Let Your Happiest Ending Lead You

It's easy to get caught up in the emotions of the moment and see the struggle in front of you as a battle that you want to hurry up, to be "done with it." What can be helpful is to take some time and space away from the situation and again imagine how you would like things to look in the future. Reference your post-divorce vision, and determine your best course of action.

The relational tone at any particular moment may be hostile and contemptuous; fueled by your exhaustion, disappointment, and frustration. It is entirely likely that these emotions are coming out, not just in your words and behavior, but in your deeper decisions. If you can imagine your preferred relational "tone" at the conclusion of your divorce, you can allow this vision to guide your words and behavior instead. It is impossible to control or predict how your partner will respond to you, as they have their own feelings and objectives, but you can do your part to set a kind and healthy tone. When you are kind, your partner might just meet you with kindness in return.

To help you increase the likelihood of an amicable divorce, I recommend you avoid *blaming, shaming,* or *criticizing* your ex. You can bring up grievances in a productive way by considering how you might gently give feedback to a close friend, work colleague, or your child. Remember that however calloused and mean they seem to be treating you in the moment, they too have feelings, and you will benefit from attempting to respect their feelings. Bringing up issues from the past is also a bad idea. As best you can, avoid arguments and mixing your old hurts into your navigation of your divorce. Try instead to *listen* to your partner and to own some part of what they see as their reality. Then attempt to share your perspective without making them "wrong." This is tricky and can be supported through reading materials designed to guide healthy communication, talking with supportive friends, and consulting with a therapist. Keep in mind people will naturally respond in defensive ways to information they are not ready to process. Trying to force your partner to see your perspective or pushing them to own aspects of their behavior will likely not serve you well in keeping things amicable.

Chapter 18 Tools:

• Remember that beyond being right, we all want to feel "heard." Review your empathic listening skills and use these to facilitate productive and healthy communication with your estranged partner.

• Remember to take a time out from one another when discussions become heated or aggressive. Give yourself time to calm down. Gather your emotions first and then your thoughts before proceeding. Using the space provided below, make a list of the topics that have been more difficult to discuss with your estranged partner. Make note of the emotions that come up for you and how you might mange those emotions to allow more productive conversations.

- Remember that you will certainly have negative emotions. Find healthy ways to release negative emotions, rather than taking them out on your ex. Jot down a few ideas of things you can do to release the negative emotions you may be feeling. Schedule time to engage in these activities soon, and regularly.

_____

_____

_____

_____

_____

_____

_____

Chapter 19

Considering Things Practically

*"New beginnings are often described as
painful endings."*

– Lao Tzu

Division of Assets

**Decide What You Must Have (Not What You Don't
Want Your Partner to Have)**

When making decisions around division of assets,
including homes, furniture, pets, and personal effects, take
time to think of what you need and what you can live
without. Don't make decisions based on what you *don't
want* your ex to have. Think about your limits and what
you are willing to compromise. Then be mindful that you
are not trying to punish or retaliate through division of the
items you have acquired together. It might be helpful to
make a list of items with categories of what you need, what
you want, and what you prefer, but could live without. This
will help you negotiate more easily if your partner has a
strong desire for an item that you only have as a
preference. Often, the things you think you want now you
will get rid of following the divorce, especially if you
acquired it only to keep your partner from having it. Items
come and go, and most can and will be replaced in time.
One way to assist you in thinking about what you value

most is to imagine you only have fifteen minutes to grab your most valued, *shared* possessions from the home. What would you take? This visualization can be helpful in initiating your detachment from your possessions.

My Personal Share: Letting Go

I remember one piece of art photography that my ex wanted, and I was quite upset about releasing it to him. I knew I couldn't replace it, though I spent hours searching high and low to find something as identical as possible. It was of a European location that I had been to many times, including once with my ex. But, I let go. It wasn't worth the fight, despite my sentimental attachment and the feelings of anger looming in the background during the moment he requested it. The truth was he deserved to have some of our art. It was only my pain that created resistance in giving it to him—pain from the tremendous loss associated with letting go of so many things as I let go of our relationship.

After experiencing way too many feelings about that piece of art, I decided I could not replace it and would need to rework the theme of the room to accommodate a new piece of art. Very shortly after I made my decision, the universe gave me an amazing gift.

One day in a store I frequented, without any intention of looking for art, I ran across a piece of art photography that had a significantly more powerful meaning for me. All my life, I had refrained from going to Venice in the hopes of going with a romantic partner (despite having been to Italy three times). On a whim one summer, while doing international therapy training I decided to do a less-than-24-hour trip to Venice by myself. I "lived it up" even with my short time: nice dinner, solo gondola ride, a little shopping—I had a blast! My decision was a liberating one, as that international trip was the time in which I came to the painful decision to end my marriage and the quick jaunt to Venice represented my empowerment to visit this "romantic" location with myself, for myself, and by myself.

> *And to be joy-filled while doing it. The piece of art I stumbled upon in the shop that day was a black-and-white view of Venice from the waterways. I hadn't looked for it, nor even considered it, and yet I loved it so much more than the piece I had lamented releasing. I was reminded that when we let something go, there is something better waiting for us around the corner.*

Another consideration here is the emotional meaning you have attached to certain objects. There are some items that have such sentimental attachment or strong memories associated with them that you will not be able to use or see them without thinking of your partner anyway. This is also true regarding the decision to remain in the family home. You may want to consider whether you wish to "start over," or be tied to the memories certain items will hold, as you move forward in your new chapter. So, while you may like the item or consider it functional for future use, you may actually find you do not wish to have it around later due to the feelings it brings up for you. I think an excellent technique to use in this case is the KonMari Method. The KonMari Method was developed by the professional organizer and renowned author of the book *The Life-Changing Magic of Tidying Up*, Marie Kondo (2014). I used this method upon moving out of the home I shared with my spouse and found it tremendously helpful. While going through all of our household items is a lengthy process, divorce requires we sort through most of our possessions anyway.

Personally, I found it a cathartic task that allowed me to be mindful in the moment while doing something productive. The simple technique of this particular concept in the book (which is certainly worth the read) is to handle or touch each item in your home and notice intently how you feel and what images and emotions arise. Whatever item does not bring you peace or joy is to be let go. Thus, the beautiful leather jacket I obtained on our last trip to Europe as a couple, with tags still attached, awaiting cooler weather, was let go. Ample art, decorations, towels, and bedding were also removed. Lucky for me, my ex did not want many household items from our shared home and was happy to take many of the items I did not want and asked for very few items that I did want. Although I was sad to let some favored items go, I felt it was fair and reasonable that he selected the items he did, since I was keeping so much of what brought me peace and joy.

This may not be the case for you. You and your partner may want many of the same things, or you may not have the option to handle the items in question, particularly if you are not residing in the space where they are housed. You may also decide that while you will ultimately release something (like wedding photos), you may not be ready to do so just yet. Be gentle with yourself in these moments.

To the best of your ability, meditate to gain clarity about the items that matter and those that do not. In the end, material items are just "things," and things have a funny way of breaking, getting lost, wearing out, or otherwise leaving our life unexpectedly. Try to keep this in mind when you are sorting through and negotiating over your "things."

How to Handle Family and Friends

It is important to consider ahead of time how you intend to communicate during the separation and divorce process with the people in your lives. It's *best* if you can come to a mutually agreed-upon understanding with your partner. If it is possible to jointly discuss your individual needs for support and your concerns around each other's disclosures, you may be able to reach an agreement you can both honor. However, as this may not be possible, you can also decide for yourself what will best serve your post-divorce vision, while still allowing you to feel supported. In other words, it is important to have a support system and a few trusted confidants to help you manage emotional upheaval and big decisions you might want to talk through. But, bending the ear of just anyone is neither wise nor beneficial.

Divorce is hard. We are often in the position of feeling anxious and conflicted when we are faced with difficult, life-altering choices. During these times, I have found *myself* seeking (consciously and unconsciously) the support and validation of others that my decision is the "right one."

The truth is, no one has the right decision for *me,* and no one else can really know what is best for *you* on *your journey.* However, it is true that selective counsel from trusted friends and other wise individuals may help you consider options and alternate perspectives. But it's worth being selective in whom you choose to confide. Building a case against your partner by vilifying them to others may make you feel better in the moment, but ultimately, it may not be in your best interest. Try to keep in mind that others are often going to say something supportive because they love you and not because you are actually "right." In fact, if your partner gave their version of the story to someone (which may feel true for them and fabricated to you), they would often be given the same kind of support. *No one actually wins by pulling more people to their side.*

While pulling people to your side during the separation and divorce may make you feel better in the moment, it often creates greater conflict as people are now involved in your business (even if you don't want them to be). Keep this in mind when seeking support from friends, family, neighbors, work associates, and others. Be particular about where you seek support and wise regarding who you choose to involve in your relationship struggles. Using caution with social media is also important. In this age, anything you put out on social media may be there forever. Making emotionally driven decisions to post on your social sites for support can create problems for you now and later. Social media posts are used by employers, attorneys and thus judges (in divorce and custody matters) and can negatively impact your relationships. If your partner really *is* awful, their actions will speak for themselves as things unfold and move forward. The universe has a way of balancing these things out. You do not need to invest your precious time and energy in ensuring your partner receives "justice" for their "crimes."

A final consideration is that it is not possible to truly understand the unique pain of what it is like to come to a decision to go through the process of a divorce unless you have experienced it firsthand. Those who have not gone through that unique form of pain may struggle to comprehend your perspective and feelings. For that matter, even if someone has divorced, no one but you can fully understand *your* marriage and divorce from *your* inside experience. Thus, try not to become too concerned or sidetracked by the perspectives and advice of those around you. Keep in mind that while their intentions may be good, their advice might not be the best option for you.

One way to reduce unsolicited questions and comments from those in your life is to make a unified announcement together, requesting your boundaries, whatever they may be, are respected. Technology has made this option a bit more accessible. Sending an email, as a couple, can inform those in your life of the decision you have reached and what type of support you would appreciate, as well as how to respect your clearly outlined boundaries. You can find an example of what this might look like on the next page.

Divorce Email Announcement Sample

Dear Friends and Family,

We are sending this email to inform you of our decision to end our marriage. It's a sad but important decision for us both and one that we do not take lightly. We acknowledge you may have questions and your own feelings about this news. Please know that we both have put in the work to arrive at this point and ask that you respect our choice.

We want to take this moment to say thank you for your continued love, compassion, advice, and support. Without you all, our relationship wouldn't have been as rich or fulfilling.

Most importantly, we would love to hear from you all going forward. We aren't interested in discussing details of our relationship, but if you'd like to check-in or connect with us as individuals, our contact information is listed below.

With love and gratitude,

Partner 1:   Partner 2:

Name   Name
Address   Address
Phone Number   Phone Number

Email   Email

Handling a Hostile Ex-Partner

Clients often come to me seeking therapy after they are emotionally spent from attempting to navigate a relationship or divorce with an argumentative and hostile partner. The sad truth is, some people just love to fight. Some people love to seek vengeance and believe it will leave them feeling better. In these cases, if you are the one committed to divorcing in love and maintaining your own sense of peace, you will work hard one way or the other. You might as well work to keep your energy in the best possible place, rather than spending energy meeting them in their aggressive state.

How you feel about yourself is the most important thing. It is not only why you are reading this book, but likely one reason why you are divorcing your partner in the first place! If you are married to a hostile partner, you most likely want to bring your life to a more peaceful, healthy, and fulfilling state. To achieve this, you must set boundaries with yourself to refrain from engaging in unproductive, emotionally charged interactions with your spouse. If they like to fight, they will likely have many tricky ways to entice you into engaging in arguments or becoming emotionally riled up. If you set boundaries about how far you are willing to allow yourself to go before you call a time out or otherwise end the interaction, you are less likely to cause damage to yourself in the divorce process. Keep in

How you feel about yourself is the most important thing.

mind that once your brain or your partner's brain is activated into fight or flight, nothing productive is going to happen. Therefore, if you have an especially difficult partner, I encourage you to use the techniques and strategies in this book to *plan*. Create a plan about the ways you will interact, the emotional cues you will use to inform you that it is time to back away from an interaction, and always plan to take *extra space* in the form of time outs when your boundaries are crossed, or you're in emotional upheaval. Using meditation and visualization, like the one below, to clear your mind and your energetic space is also helpful. It may be helpful to keep in mind that individuals who like to fight use enticing statements as a manipulative distraction to side-track the conversation from the intended topic, especially if they are in the hot seat. If you keep this in mind, you may be more inclined to ignore this coercive strategy and stay on track with your conversational goal.

Exercise Invitation: Acting "As If"

What would happen if...we imagined a struggle was already solved? Sometimes, we can become so preoccupied with an issue that we find it difficult to function effectively in other areas of life. When we encounter emotional struggles which we have limited or no control over, "acting as if" is an effective way to get through the challenge.

To be clear, I am not suggesting you avoid handling real life matters, like caring for your children or paying your bills. But give yourself a break from difficulties that plague your mind, so that you can move your emotions into a more positive space and your energy into a more effective and productive mode.

For this exercise, draw a line through the middle of a piece of paper. On one side, write down the problem which troubles you. On the other side, write down a fantasized realistic solution. Now close your eyes and imagine what it would feel like if this were truly the case. Notice how you feel in your body.

Allow yourself to breathe in the relief, happiness, or peace your solution brings. Then exhale and decide it is so.

Allow yourself to hold this image vividly in your mind for a few minutes before opening your eyes.

Let yourself begin working toward that goal by acting as though it is already the case. As Melody Beattie shares in *The Language of Letting Go* (1990), "Acting as if is a positive way to overcome fear, doubts, and low self-esteem. We do not have to lie; we do not have to be dishonest with ourselves.

We open up to the positive possibilities of the future, instead of limiting the future by today's feelings and circumstances." In most situations, we lack the direct control to change things to be as we wish. So why not imagine the best possible outcome? We will have to deal with the resulting outcome regardless of whether it goes as we hoped, but wasting time feeling the pain of it going badly robs us of today for a tomorrow that may never come.

If, on the other hand, you are the one in the relationship who feels drawn to create drama and instigate fights, I would encourage you to seek professional support and guidance while you use this book. Additionally, I would suggest you consider using the revenge exercise on the following page to help you play out your fantasy *one time*, so that you may let it go and more quickly move into the healing space of forgiveness. Sometimes, even if we have a greater desire to operate from a loving place, our pain and our learned behaviors can lead us to behave in unhealthy and unproductive ways. This is when we can choose to implement a bit of compassion as we call upon our strength to make better choices.

Exercise Invitation: Revel in Revenge

I only suggest you engage in this if you are struggling to let go of your desire for your ex to suffer for their "crimes." Typically, it is best to move forward into a positive space where your ex and your emotions are concerned. But if you find yourself wanting bad things to happen to your ex-partner, allow yourself to momentarily own that feeling. Let yourself fully embrace the fantasies you have for revenge, before you commit to letting go and moving on to forgiveness.

Not everyone will feel a need to do this, but if you are currently in this negative emotional space, simply accept it as it is.

In this exercise, set a timer for 5-10 minutes. In that time, allow your mind to play out all of the "punishments" you believe your ex is due. <u>You are only intended to do this exercise once</u>, so decide what it is you need to get out of your system. When you have finished your designated time, set your fantasies aside and pick one of the other forgiveness exercises to complete. This last step is important—both to help you release your previous negative thoughts, and to move you into a different emotional space...and on toward the healing work of forgiveness.

Chapter 19 Tools:

- When considering division of tangible shared items, make a list of the things you need, want, and would like, but could feasibly live without. You will likely require more than space provided below to make a comprehensive list.

- Consider using the KonMari Method to sort through items in your home and release things that do not bring you joy. This is one way to reduce holding on to items which you will later release.

- Determine (with your estranged partner if possible) how you will handle sharing information with mutual friends and family. Keep in mind that support is important, but bashing your ex is unnecessary. Avoid bringing others to your side of the fight against your ex!

- If you are navigating divorce with a hostile partner, remind yourself each day how you want to feel about yourself. Write down some key words below to remind you how you want to feel about yourself. Do your best not to be pulled into behavior that will later leave you feeling badly. Try your best to hold your boundaries.

_____

_____

_____

_____

_____

_____

Section IV

HEALING IN THE AFTERMATH

Some of our most valuable life lessons come from our most difficult experiences. This is unfortunate, but true. One of my most influential doctoral professors, Dr. David Elkins, shared his existentially-based thoughts on the ups and downs of life in his book *Beyond Religion* when he wrote, "Life is more than climbing mountains and overcoming the next challenge. Life is also about going down, descending into the valleys, and experiencing the pain and tragedies of life. We need a spirituality that can support us not only when we are planting our flag at the top of the mountain but also when we have fallen off the mountain or cannot even find the courage to begin the climb" (1998). His sentiment is a powerful one that highlights the precious value of leaning on our higher power or our best self during difficult times. Because no matter how we try to avoid "falling down," we are guaranteed to fall from time to time.

I recall numerous occasions throughout my life calling my father to share my most recent disappointment, failure, or struggle, only to hear his standard conclusion that this was "just another one of those life lessons." What felt like a pat response was frustrating at times, humorous at others, and ultimately, it was a relief. The very sincere message he was trying to convey was simple: *Life will most certainly not go as you hope. But in every experience, there is an*

213

opportunity for growth. Your divorce process is no different. This time of confusion, pain, and strife is the perfect time for you to explore and implement the life lessons being offered. Allow this time to be one that benefits you, as you practice moving in the direction of love. Well-known author, activist, spiritual leader, and politician Marianne Williamson states in her life-changing book, *A Return to Love* (1992), "It takes courage...to endure the sharp pains of self-discovery rather than choose to take the dull pain of unconsciousness that would last the rest of our lives" So, as you move forward in this book, I encourage you to call upon the courageous Heart Warrior within you. Learn to love yourself a bit more as you attempt to love those around you—even if you don't like them very much!

> *I encourage you to call upon the courageous heart warrior within you.*

Chapter 20

Fostering Forgiveness

*"We may need to get mad for a while as we search for what
could have been to finally accept what is."*

– Melody Beattie

Understanding Forgiveness

Forgiveness can be tricky. If you were to imagine forgiving
your partner at this moment, what would you feel? For
many people, the idea of forgiveness is met with some
initial resistance—particularly if they have been wronged
by someone they trusted and loved. Sometimes we don't
want to forgive, because we believe this is the same as
saying what happened or what was done to us is "okay."
Forgiveness and condoning someone's bad behavior is not
the same. Forgiveness is also not something that happens
because our negative feelings about the issue have gone
away or because we stopped thinking about the pain we
feel.

The first step toward forgiveness is acknowledging your
willingness to forgive. Until you are willing to let go, you
will not. The next step is to learn to think about your upset
in a new way—to recall it differently (Worthington 2003).
When we forgive, we are making a conscious decision
(sometimes again and again...and again) to let go of the
negative thoughts we are holding and release the emotions

as they arise, so that we can move forward from our previously held ideas and memory of the experience. Whether you simply let your thoughts go, or do the deeper work of challenging your beliefs to reframe them as personal preferences, rather than universal rules of engagement, shifting your current pattern of thought is essential.

Divorce is a decision to end one part of our life in hopes of moving on to something healthier, more supportive, and fitting with our vision for our life. This is an entirely realistic goal, and I believe it is important to remember things will get better in time. However, *it is not possible to move forward without first letting go of our past pain and suffering.* Forgiveness is your path to letting go and moving on. Forgiveness is key to a healthy existence. I would encourage you to consider working through forgiveness regularly, whether you plan to divorce or hope to reconcile your marriage.

My Personal Share: "Bug Food"

I'd like to share a symbolic personal story about when I discovered my ability to let go and move forward.

While I was nearing my decision to divorce and in a great deal of emotional strife, I spent a considerable amount of time finding solace in my vegetable garden. Gardening was a relatively new hobby that I began a few years prior, and it was a major part of my life.

I tended to my organic vegetables daily, pruning plants, nourishing them with supplements, removing parasites, deterring birds and squirrels, and supporting the overall growth of more and more varieties of plants. I studied all things gardening— read books and articles, took classes, exchanged ideas with friends and neighbors, and was delighted, in a highly geeked-out way, every time I prepared a meal from my organic garden.

I realized later that in the absence of being able to start a family, this garden was absorbing a great deal of my nurturing energy, and as such, I was highly attached to it. I experienced my garden as a refuge when I needed an escape from the tensions of the household and a source of validation when I was not receiving any in my marriage.

Early on in my marriage and my gardening, my husband had sprayed the plants with pesticide while he was treating the yard. I was outraged! We had in-depth conversations about how this was not okay because I was spending so much time (and money) caring for my garden without toxins. At that time, it was an honest mistake on his part, and he simply hadn't thought it through. Based on my outrage, it was an accident he was clearly not going to repeat.

Flash to the spring of our separation. I entered my garden one afternoon to find "bug food" pellets sprinkled throughout the garden. Plant leaves were covered in little blue pellets, and the ground was generously peppered with them as well. What is "bug food," you might wonder? This was the name my husband continued to repeat back to me when I asked why he put pesticide on my garden. "It's not pesticide," he would retort, "it's bug food." The outrage and pain I felt about his choice to do this— which felt deliberate based on his assertion that it was food for bugs—was visceral.

Rather than apologizing or taking ownership, he decidedly held his stance that it was bug food—causing an all-out fight in which I, in my crazed state of mind, retrieved the "bug food" bag he had concealed in the alleyway trash can to unnecessarily prove my point that he had "poisoned" my organic garden.

In despair and heartache, I went to the internet. I began posting on gardening sites to gather information on what I might do to combat this action and "clean up" my organic garden. I do not recall what I said, but I have no doubt my emotional upset came through dramatically on my post. I received much sympathy and some warnings against eating anything from the garden.

I also received one response with the most helpful advice imaginable. HippyGal1950 replied: "Dear Becca, I am so saddened to hear of your gardening upset. In the absence of understanding why he did this, we should only assume he had good but misguided intentions. Despite the pain you now feel for your garden, the good news is you, much like your garden, will transcend this setback."

Her words spoke directly to my soul and were exactly what I needed to hear in that moment. I emailed HippyGal1950 outside of the gardening chat room to thank her for getting my head back on straight. She was right, and this lesson in wisdom stuck with me both through my divorce and beyond. Rather than fixating on what he had done to upset me, I chose to feel the pain and let it go, to forgive, even though he did not seek forgiveness. This was the only path to transcendence.

I did transcend that experience, including the pain of being in what I experienced as a lonely, hostile marriage. And I went on to garden elsewhere—taking several plants from that garden into the garden of my next home, where both I and my garden flourished.

Forgiveness Is a Choice

As I mentioned in the bug food example, forgiveness is not the same thing as promoting or excusing the things you or your partner did. And forgiveness doesn't happen by accident, it is a choice we make. My decision to forgive my husband did not mean I was immediately without feelings when I thought of what had occurred. But each time they arose, I used my self-talk to coach myself through it. For

> *Rather than fixating on what he had done to upset me, I chose to feel the pain and let it go; to forgive, even though he did not seek forgiveness.*

example, "What's done is done. Let it go." Or, "He doesn't know how else to communicate his feelings with you right now, this is not about you. Let it go." As I made the choice each time to let it go, the pain moved further and further away from me. The *willingness* to forgive is a major factor in the effectiveness of this process.

The case for forgiveness is that it allows us space to move forward, let go of our anger, and find our inner peace. When we forgive, we are freeing our partner and ourselves from our negative feelings, or energy. By doing so, we are also removing our partner's (intentional or unintentional) emotional hold over us.

We do not have to deny our own pain and hurt to forgive our ex-spouse. In fact, our pain may be helpful by bringing us more in touch with how we may have grown or helping us identify areas in which we still need to grow. Remember, we are all flawed and less than perfect. We most often learn and grow in relationships...and they are not always the easiest or most comfortable lessons. Our healthiest learning and growth occurs when we take the emotional risk of making ourselves vulnerable while learning where to set boundaries to protect ourselves. As you begin to work through forgiveness, you may find areas in which your anger is misdirected and would be better

221

directed toward yourself for not identifying, communicating, or asserting your own boundaries and needs. If you find the forgiveness process too difficult to navigate on your own, I would encourage you to seek support with a professional—a psychotherapist, counselor, or trained spiritual leader.

> *"Resentment is like drinking poison and then hoping it will kill your enemies."*
>
> – Nelson Mandela

The idea of forgiving your partner in the midst of the separation, divorce, or contemplation of divorce may seem like an impossible task. The heightened emotional experience associated with this time period can be overwhelming. Typically, it is fueled by unresolved and seemingly unresolvable conflict.

Therapeutic Invitation:

Take a moment now to consider the discord between you and your partner and then scan your body. You might notice tightness in your stomach, jaw, or throat; heaviness in your chest; a headache; or some other unpleasant physical symptoms. Those physical symptoms are informing you that the experiences you've gone through are not pleasant or desirable. However, the emotions associated with these physical feelings are important, causing us to draw our attention inward. They help us tune into our personal experience and then hopefully make necessary adjustments to bring our life more in line with our true needs and desires. Working on forgiveness by using our emotions and feelings as a roadmap of hurts to be healed is an important step in getting your life closer to where you want it—to a more peaceful and healthy state. Make a list of some of the things you would like to be able to let go (one day) though forgiveness of your partner:

_____

_____

_____

_____

_____

_____

_____

While emotions (even the ones deemed "negative") are important in life, chronically experiencing negative feelings are detrimental to your health. In fact, there are toxic effects to holding onto anger and resentment like physical stress, which leads to more serious issues such as stroke and heart attack. Depressed immune function and thus exposure to increased infections and communicable disease can also occur when we retain stress in the form of negative emotions. Further, the mental stress of holding on to your negative emotions exacerbates depression, anxiety, and PTSD, while disrupting supportive self-care behaviors like adequate sleep and a healthy appetite. *Reflect back on the physical experiences you felt in your body as you were asked in the last paragraph to consider past negative interactions with your estranged partner. Now recognize how these feelings compile and compound over months and years of unresolved and unforgiven hurts.*

While forgiving your ex-partner may sound like the worst idea, just making the decision to work toward forgiving them can actually improve your health. Studies have found benefits in this across multiple major markers of physical health, including reduction of negative physical symptoms, decreased amount of medications used, improved sleep quality, and reduction of fatigue.

All of this research begs the question: *Why hold on to negative emotions and detrimental physical symptoms longer than necessary?* I continue to assert that negative emotions are healthy, purposeful, and *necessary.* But carrying them around after they are no longer useful is pointless and destructive. When you hold on to old emotions caused by your ex's words and behaviors, **you are causing damage to yourself.** In this line of thought, forgiveness is actually for *you*, not for the person you forgive. Most of the time, any person we believe has wronged us has already put the transgression out of their mind. We are the one carrying it around—like a giant weight we are dragging through life. Now is the time to drop that weight and begin living the life you want: lighter, freer, and more peaceful.

Forgiveness actually for you, not for the person

Why Not Seek Revenge?

If you are open to contemplating forgiveness but find your mind pulling you toward fantasies or plans of revenge...that's okay, relax—you're only human. Thoughts of revenge can be considered a natural state of mind. In my therapeutic experiences, many people find themselves exploring fantasies of revenge upon which they will never act. Michael E. McCullough, a University of Miami professor, argues that the revenge response is evolutionary, suggesting that it kept early humans safe by deterring would-be enemies from harming them[2]. What's more, it may actually make you feel better in the moment, as simply fantasizing about revenge for an extended period activates the dorsal striatum in the brain, the same part

---

[2] McCullough, Kurzban, and Tabak, 2010

stimulated by sex and chocolate. When economists from the University of Zurich uncovered this in 2004, they proposed that this kick in our brain incentivizes us to seek revenge, even if *the ultimate cost comes at our own expense*[3], much like eating too much chocolate might. That is an important factor to co   el toward revenge is a product   *Revenge may give you* chemical releases in your brai   *temporary relief from* which brings you a tempora   *your pain now, but* feeling of relief from your pai   *will not leave you*   *feeling better in the* It is important that you pu   *long run.* back for a moment and consid the long-term ramifications of   ay give you temporary relief from your pain now, but it will not leave you feeling better in the long run.

While revenge certainly is an option, the question is whether it will ultimately serve you, your health, your spouse, your divorce outcome, or if applicable, your children. Studies suggest it will not[4]. The *fleeting* fantasy of revenge, maintained as a passing thought rather than an obsessive one, may serve as a supportive coping behavior by offering temporary relief. However, the *act* of "getting even" with your estranged partner ultimately perpetuates your experience of negative emotions, like

---

[3] De Quervain et al., 2004

[4]Carlsmith, Wilson, and Gilbert, 2008

anger, guilt, and shame, and may leave you holding greater negative energy than you had prior to acting on the revenge. If you feel your desire for revenge is impeding your ability to move forward toward forgiveness, you might consider taking a moment to utilize the revenge fantasy exercise for forgiveness in Section V to assist you in moving along in your emotional processing and toward your post-divorce vision.

Self-Awareness Requires Courage

I have had countless clients assert their willingness to forgive *only if* the other person was willing to apologize first. If you feel you are willing to forgive but only if your estranged partner apologizes, you might be allowing your path to freedom to be interrupted by your partner's lack of self-awareness. Your ex may have limited recognition or understanding of how they have wronged you; they may have what is referred to in psychotherapy as "low ego strength." *Ego strength* accounts for our resilience in difficult situations, and those with higher ego strength tend to have higher emotional intelligence. Emotional intelligence, a term made popular by researcher Daniel Goleman, can be understood as one's capacity to manage one's own emotions, as well as the emotions of others. If your partner lacks the *insight* to examine the ways their behavior has hurt you—they likely have a low EQ *capacity*. Or, they may simply lack the *courage* to face the negative feelings within themselves and those which they have caused you by their behavior. If your ex lacks the courage necessary for self-awareness, do not let this deter or block your progress toward your post-divorce vision!

Owning mistakes is more difficult for some than others. You may know (or have married) someone who struggles to say "I'm sorry" regardless of how obvious their culpability seems. These people, in my experience, are those that feel overloaded with shame when owning fault in a situation, and thus, avoid their responsibility to make amends. To be clear, we all make mistakes and hurt others, knowingly and unknowingly. You and your partner are no exception. But ultimately, what you may be holding on to is really disappointment about what they lack in ego strength or courage. It may be their inability to fully *acknowledge* that they've hurt you that fuels your anger, rather than the behaviors or events they have perpetrated against you (albeit those were likely wrong as well).

It is my suspicion that if you reflect back on your relationship, your partner's frustrating personality was present throughout your marriage. You may now be struggling with the reality of who you selected as your life partner and how they operate in the world. Rather than some particular bad behavior that hurt or disrespected you, you may now be realizing you compromised yourself for your relationship in ways you wished you hadn't. You might even find that deep beneath your disappointment with your partner is anger with yourself for not knowing how their unfavorable character traits would ultimately hurt you. Perhaps, you are angry with yourself for not handling things differently to protect yourself. Your work in this case is to be *honest* about who you picked as a life partner. In some way, for some reason, this person appeared to fit you at the time of your decision. Typically, this is because there was some way you needed to grow— something you needed to learn about yourself from the relationship. Learn to accept that this person is who you chose to marry, and accept their limitations as part of their humanness. Let go of expecting something other than who they are and what they can realistically give you at this time. This is not the same thing as learning to *like* who they are or how they behave, but only to accept it and stop hoping in vain for a different response during marriage, divorce, or beyond.

> *You might even find that deep beneath your disappointment with your partner, is anger with yourself for not knowing how these character traits would ultimately hurt you.*

Something to consider: we often attribute to others the perspectives that we ourselves possess, assuming others must also have our same awareness and abilities. But I can tell you firsthand, as a psychologist, that everyone's brain operates differently. The skills you have personally developed and the way you perceive situations may not align with how others function and see things, particularly, in this case, your ex. The fact is, your ex may not be willing or able, at this time, to recognize and address the issues you would like them to address. In lieu of their courage to change, you can still choose to show up as a Heart Warrior—to detach from them with love and free yourself from the bondage of your anger. The choice to find that freedom is yours alone. You can do this through forgiveness.

Visualization Invitation: Storybook Release

Imagine yourself as a small child reading a colorful storybook. Picture yourself turning the pages. Imagine brightly colored illustrations depicting your life with your partner. Start from the beginning of your relationship when you first met. Continue to look through your dating, engagement, and marriage.

Be sure to notice the positive experiences as well as the negative. As you do this, notice the feelings that arise within you and just allow them to be what they are. If you feel happiness, smile or laugh. If you feel sadness or hurt, allow yourself to cry.

Now notice someone is sitting next to you and has been reading along in the same illustrated storybook. It is the child version of your ex-partner, and you realize they have been crying and smiling right along with you. Notice how it feels to share this experience and how you feel about them as you imagine them being impacted just as you are by these same shared life experiences. This may be hard, but try to stay with it. When you finish the exercise, notice how you feel about your ex-partner in the moment and whether your feelings have changed from when you first began. The truth is, we are all sharing a human experience and doing our best in each moment. Try to keep in mind that your ex had hopes of things working out differently in their mind as well.

Managing Personal Guilt

I often encounter people blaming their partners for their marriage ending, citing some transgression as the cause.

As a psychologist (and a divorced person), I do not believe marriages end because of an act of cheating or other such wrongdoing. I believe that in most cases cheating and deception are the result of an already broken marital structure. One in which healthy communication has broken down (if it was ever present to begin with) and emotional intimacy has been lost or was never developed in the first place. Transgressions, like cheating and deception, tend to happen in a kind of layering effect. Negative circumstances and interactions pile up in the marital relationship, and one or both partners look for some escape from the stress. Often, the mode of escape is familiar to that person from before the marriage—lying, substance abuse, excessive spending, sexually acting out (pornography, strip clubs, infidelity, etc.), or turning inappropriately to another relationship. Additionally, in an effort to avoid inner discomfort or marital conflict, partners may begin to avoid seeking connection with one another or physically avoid one-on-one time altogether (becoming busy with time-consuming hobbies, traveling for work, or spending time with friends). This disconnection leads to further miscommunication and misunderstanding.

Sometimes, it is the "final straw" of violence, cheating, or deception that brings the marital dysfunction to a head. On other occasions, couples become so detached that physically walking away from the marriage is just a formality, as they left it mentally and emotionally long before. Either way, many people are making independent or self-serving decisions long before the conversation of ending the marriage takes place. In these situations, their behaviors may serve to create guilt. Sometimes that guilt creeps in immediately at the time of the behavior. Other times, it only arises once partners have taken space from the critical state of their failing marriage.

While we are often deeply hurt and angry with our partner by the time we consider divorce, it can also be the case that our upset has led us, by that point, to make life choices about which we carry guilt. Many clients express guilt around the affair they had, the secret life they created, their horrible outbursts of anger, or the financial deception in which they engaged. Guilt is a healthy emotion that serves an important purpose, to inform us when we are going against our values or harming others. However, once we have received the intended message and decided the best way to respond the situation (discontinue the behavior, make amends, learn from our mistakes, etc.), it is no longer useful to hold on to it. Regardless of how upsetting your past behavior may be for you now, it is necessary to move forward from it and into the present. To move on from guilt you must reflect on your misstep, change your way of thinking that allowed you to take that misstep, determine how you will handle things differently in the future, and use that information to grow and evolve...as we were all meant to do. If needed, we can make amends to those we have harmed. Then, we must let it go. Holding on to guilt past the point of productivity only serves to impede our future behavior. It complicates our future decisions and sets us up to make poor choices, from a place of guilt. Inappropriately holding on to guilt prevents us from setting boundaries or believing we deserve good things and can move us into a state of shame (and you recall from Section II how damaging shame can be). Regardless of where you find yourself in this moment of divorce consideration or process, working through your guilt and allowing self-forgiveness is important for your healing.

The human psyche is fascinating. Often, when we feel an emotion, it gets twisted and tangled and comes out as another emotion entirely. Our denied emotions can even show up in our perception as though they belong to someone else (this is the psychological term *projection*). In other words, if you feel angry, you might interpret someone else's behavior as coming from a place of anger. This is why it is important to recognize and process your emotions. The last thing you need is to be stuck in a feedback loop of anger because you're not forgiving yourself and thus are perceiving those around you as angry.

Self-forgiveness will benefit you in your health, family, career, future relationships, and divorce process. In fact, even if you believe your partner's behavior was "worse" than your own, you may still hold guilt about your responsibility for your own bad behavior. Coming to a place of forgiveness is a way of creating a "clean slate" from which you have a better opportunity of taking care of yourself and communicating with your ex (and other individuals) in a more productive manner.

Exercise Invitation:
Self-Forgiveness Mirror Work

This exercise can be very powerful and bring up some deep emotions if done in earnest. For this mirror exercise, you will need yourself and a mirror. It might be easiest to stand in front of a mirror, but you can use a hand mirror as well. You can best support this exercise by first making a list of the things about which you are upset with yourself (i.e., I did not hold my boundaries about our finances; I did not confront my partner's affairs, despite knowing about them; I knew this was not a healthy relationship and got married anyway; I didn't seek the support I needed and instead acted out in my marriage, etc.). Making a list helps you to focus on what runs through you mind and serves to keep you locked in your feelings of guilt and shame. However, you do not always need a list. You can do this exercise any time, on the fly, without a list. and accept myself."

For your practice, look into your eyes in the mirror and say, "I completely forgive myself for [insert item here]," or "Even though I [insert something about which you are upset with yourself], I still love and accept myself.

For example, "I completely forgive myself for acting out of anger today," or "Even though I lied to my spouse, I still love and accept myself." Repeat each sentence three times and then quietly look yourself in your eyes for several seconds as you notice what you feel. Let the truth of your experience sit with you and just notice.

You may find this difficult; you might find it's hard to believe yourself. Do it anyway. You are not making your transgressions okay; you are freeing yourself from the binds of guilt and shame. In time, you will feel the benefits of this exercise, and you will find it easier to believe yourself and to truly forgive.

Seeking Forgiveness

In addition to forgiving yourself, it may be appropriate for you to seek forgiveness from your ex. Again, even if you believe your transgressions were less significant than theirs, you likely still missed the mark on a few occasions. Is it possible an apology is in order for your negative contributions? This is a place for you to dig deep—recognize that you will feel better clearing your own conscience by owning up to your mistakes.

Gary Chapman is best known for his book, *The Five Love Languages (1992)*, which outlines the different ways people give and receive love through their behavior. Each unique behavior is referred to as a "love language," and the importance of understanding your language and the languages of those in your life is the focus of the book. This is a "must read" book for any person that values connection. Dr. Chapman has also conducted studies on preferred styles of forgiveness, referred to as someone's "Apology Language." In his book *The Five Languages of Apology (2002),* He suggests five styles of forgiveness, including expression of regret, acceptance of responsibility, making restitution, genuinely repenting, and requesting forgiveness. It is important to keep in mind that just as with love, we each express and receive forgiveness differently. Regardless of your own language, you can facilitate the forgiveness process by doing your best to determine your ex-partner's language. (It is also helpful to know your own.) With this information, you will be better equipped to offer a meaningful apology to your partner and, if they're willing, assist them in seeking forgiveness from you in a meaningful manner.

If your partner is willing, consider asking them to take a quiz by Gary Chapman online to determine the best way to apologize. If they are not open to this, you may want to read his book, or take the quiz to familiarize yourself with the content and then spend some time considering which types of apologies have worked well in the past so that your attempt will be more successful. You can find the Apology Language Quiz at: 5lovelanguages.com, under the "Apology" tab.

Exercise Invitation: Set Yourself Free

Because you are human, there are likely ways you have hurt or harmed your partner that create an opportunity for seeking forgiveness. Taking ownership over your own contributions is a powerful tool in the process of healing and obtaining closure. You may want to take some time to revisit (and possibly document) the timeline of your marriage, while taking an honest look at the places you did not shine your brightest. Write down some areas or incidents in which you could have been kinder, more supportive, more accepting, or more loving to your partner, and then decide if you would benefit from forgiving yourself alone or from seeking forgiveness from your ex. You might place a check mark next to those which you would like to seek forgiveness directly. If you do not have a safe or receptive ex, you can imagine or visualize a conversation in which you ask for their forgiveness and imagine them receiving your request with love and kindness.

_____

_____

_____

_____

_____

_____

_____

Compassion to Facilitate Forgiveness

Perhaps one of the simplest paths to forgiveness is admitting that we are all human, we are flawed, and we have caused pain to others. Regardless of how we value or rate the level of pain we may have caused in comparison to that we have experienced at the hands of our partner, *we have all caused others pain.* Though we may be aware of some of the hurt, we likely do not have an accurate perception of the pain we have caused others whether intentionally or unintentionally. It is safe to say some have been hurt by us and never let us know. When we accidentally or reactively cause pain to others, we may find it easy to believe that we are deserving of forgiveness. As the saying goes, ***we judge others by their worst***

240

behavior and ourselves by our best intentions. Others deserve our compassion as much as we deserve compassion. Despite the nature of the error they made, compassion and forgiveness are possible if you are open and willing.

Regardless of your justification for choosing to forgive your ex, forgiveness will set you free from bringing negativity with you into your next relationship. Forgiveness is usually not as simple as turning a switch off. Forgiveness is a process—letting go of our anger over and over until it fully releases. There may be multiple layers and feelings that can be sorted out over time. This is when a therapist can be especially helpful in facilitating your process.

As a therapist, I have often been asked when someone will know when they have fully forgiven another. My answer is, when you can genuinely wish your ex well and no longer feel pain in your heart or a gnawing feeling in your stomach (or other such unpleasant physical reaction). This open and relaxed state of positive energy is usually a sign we have fully forgiven that person. However, there may be layers to your pain and thus your forgiveness process. You may need to release certain aspects of your pain, while other thoughts still cause anger, until you have fully worked your way to total forgiveness. For some, this process may extend long past

> *I was aware that remaining in a state of emotional turmoil kept me prisoner to the very marriage I had chosen to leave.*

your divorce. Regardless of your own personal process, which may be influenced by a multitude of variables including timing, nature of the offending behavior, and ease with which you can let go of your ruminating thoughts, *forgiveness is possible and necessary for your mental and emotional health.*

My Personal Share: Forgiveness

In my personal divorce experience, I continued to hear unsolicited, upsetting information about my ex-husband long after we were divorced. The behavior my ex engaged in during our marriage, about which I was previously unaware, was repeatedly brought to my attention in casual social settings. In the beginning, these painful "news updates" stung and caused a surge of negative emotions and physical feelings in me. In time, I was less impacted by the information I learned, and later on, I became better at stopping people in their tracks before they could disclose information that I did not want to hear.

This was a deliberate act of self-love on my part that seemed to confuse or shock others who appeared certain I would be interested in continuing to hear the gossip of my ex's life, including his behavior during our marriage and separation, as well as after finalization of divorce. I knew that in order to fully forgive, I had to stop seeking reasons to hold on to my pain. What I did not know about my ex's behavior during our marriage no longer mattered and only hindered my own ability to move on with my life. I was aware that remaining in a state of emotional turmoil kept me prisoner to the very marriage I had chosen to leave. I instead took responsibility for my emotional freedom.

I encourage you to engage in the exercises throughout this chapter, which is focused on forgiveness. Investing time working toward the release of your accumulated pain is a major factor in your ability to free yourself. It is possible to be in the midst of a negative experience and choose to hold on to your positive emotional energy. But it requires practice—attainable through these exercises. Whether you struggle with these exercises or are able to complete them on your own, you may find therapeutic assistance useful as you work toward forgiveness and finding your inner peace.

Seeking assistance from a therapist (especially one who specializes in facilitating an active healing process, rather than allowing you to spin repeatedly in your past pain) can be particularly useful during this time. If you choose to navigate the grief and forgiveness process on your own or with the support of a trusted confidant, there are some important interventions you may want to consider. Something very important to develop is awareness and management of your cognitions (specifically being able to notice and sort through which thoughts are helpful and which are hurtful to you). Additionally, focusing on emotional repair and spiritual work will be highly supportive to your personal growth during this time.

Chapter 20 Tools:

- Forgiveness and condoning someone's bad behavior are not the same thing. We do not need to agree with someone's actions to make a decision to forgive them and let go. Our willingness to forgive is the first step, so if you are not yet ready to work on forgiving, begin to move toward a "willingness" to forgive and let that lead you. Remember, it is not possible to move forward in a healthy manner until you have first released the past.

- Even if there was a "final straw" that brought you to consider divorce, it is rarely *that action* that "caused" the divorce. Take some time to both reflect on and write down what you and your partner contributed that led to the marriage becoming unhealthy and disconnected. This information is beneficial to your personal growth, rather than merely finding fault with your partner.

- Use compassion to allow you to forgive yourself for whatever you might discover. If you have hurt your partner, consider if, when, and how you might seek forgiveness for these actions.

- Keep in mind that we judge others by their worst behavior and ourselves by our best intentions. Use the exercises on the following pages to assist you in moving further through forgiveness.

_____

_____

_____

_____

_____

_____

Exercise Invitation:
Focusing on Forgiveness

Let's explore some exercises to further facilitate forgiveness. Remember that forgiveness happens on a spectrum. Prior to completing an exercise, check in with yourself to evaluate where you are mentally and emotionally. It is not an either "I have forgiven," or "I have not forgiven" situation. Create a scale in which you can rank your emotional experience using a 0 to 10 rating. In this case, 0 is having no trace of negative feeling, and 10 stands for the most significant and overwhelming experience of negative feeling you can imagine. Prior to each forgiveness exercise, write down the number you are feeling, and after completing the exercise, write down the number associated with your current level of negative feeling. In time, with continued work, you will see your number trending downward toward zero. Do not be alarmed if occasionally your number does not move down or even goes up. Working through your emotions is a process, and sometimes, you will feel worse before you feel better. Keep in mind, forgiveness is a gift you give yourself as well as your ex. It is the only way to truly free yourself from your past.

Exercise Invitation:
Freedom through Forgiveness

1. On a large sheet of paper, take 10–25 minutes to list some of the hurts you have experienced from your ex. This list can be as exhaustive as you'd like, filled with small and large upsets. You may refer back to some of the incidents you have already documented in earlier exercises. Once you have your list, break the hurts down into categories or themes (i.e., dishonesty, unkind words, control, neglect) and circle each category.

2. Sit in silence for 10–15 minutes and contemplate the deeper motivation of your ex-partner's behavior. Dig deep here. Rather than painting them as a villain and you as an innocent victim in your mind, choose to see the fear, insecurity, hurt, shame, guilt, or ignorance behind their behavior. Consider for a moment their life experiences, trauma, childhood family background, and any mental illness or personality disorder they or their family may have had. Consider how your actions might have been received or interpreted by them in the absence of their ability to read your mind. Again, dig deep. This is just for you and your healing. You do not have to share your awareness with them or anyone else.

Recall the work you have been doing up to this point to increase your compassion, even if it is a tiny amount. Give whatever compassion you can. Once you have gained some insight, move into a space of compassion for how they might have been feeling during the times they hurt you. You are then ready for the final step.

3. *Say out loud:*

_____, I forgive you for _____. I now have a deeper understanding of why you hurt me. I will no longer be hurt by you and will uphold my boundaries to take care of myself in a loving way. I am not condoning your behavior or making it okay, but I refuse to let it hold power over me any longer. I release you and move forward in a healthy and happy way.

Repeat steps 2 and 3 of this exercise as often as necessary until you are able to genuinely wish your ex-partner well.

Exercise Invitation:
Proclaiming Your Forgiveness

Imagine the scale (0-10) while saying aloud, "I forgive (your ex's name)." Notice how, with practice, this number shifts from higher to lower as you simply repeat the sentence and consider the idea of forgiveness.

Chapter 21

Owning Your Growth Opportunities

"In the middle of difficulty lies opportunity."

– Unknown

Watching Your Thoughts

Becoming mindful of your cognitions, or self-talk, is tremendously important for your personal healing and forgiveness journey. You must be aware of your *self-talk*— made up of the automatic thoughts and core beliefs you developed from your life experiences—so you can correct any damaging or limiting beliefs at their base level. In fact, it is crucial for mental wellness that you begin to notice and work with shifting your own imprisoning or limiting thoughts. Challenging your negative thoughts and beliefs and reframing them into healthier statements has tremendous impact on your emotional state. It directly influences your self-perception, your perception of those around you, and of the world at large. Interestingly, adjusting to more productive thoughts can positively impact your *physical health* as well.

Once you are mindfully aware enough to see your thought patterns, you can begin to intervene from a place of compassionate curiosity. Interventions offered by therapists work with unhelpful thoughts which includes some form of *Thought Stopping, Cognitive Challenging,* and *Cognitive Reframing.* These are techniques to help change the automatic negative patterns of your mind and the resulting negative emotions you experience. *Thought Stopping* is the process of interrupting and removing or discontinuing an unproductive train of thought. Ideally, this is done as early as possible, once we are aware we have been thinking unproductively. It is far easier to stop the momentum of our thoughts before they have taken us over completely. Just as it is easier to stop a person from knocking us over if they are walking toward us, rather than running at full speed. *Cognitive Challenging* asks that you "poke holes" in or dispute your beliefs by considering that they might not be true, and *Cognitive Reframing* offers a way to look at your thoughts or beliefs from an alternate perspective, to see them in a new way. One of my clients refers to this as "shifting my head five degrees" and is pleased to report things look entirely different, despite nothing having changed. By using these relatively simple techniques, you can begin to change your view of reality and how you feel about things in your world. ***When we choose a different perspective, our emotions will shift.***

Therapeutic Invitation:

Try to imagine yourself driving down the highway. Suddenly, you are cut off by a fast-moving car. You feel your body's visceral response kick in, and you are charged with energy. Often, we automatically become angry after this primitive fear response kicks in, and we have an urge to confront the driver (verbally, physically, or mentally). We often make an assumption that this person is careless or selfish or otherwise intentional in their behavior and disregard for our safety. However, if we can reframe the situation by extending compassion (i.e., I have likely been careless, distracted, or hurried in my own driving and startled others), we create a different emotional experience, and our physical feelings quickly follow. Or we can choose to make up an alternative story to our automatic thought (i.e., Maybe, this person is rushing to the hospital because their wife is in labor with their first child), and we will literally feel different in our bodies.

The reality is, despite how probable we believe our story to be, it is only a story. Either way, we are making up a story about a situation or person and choosing to believe it. In this example, either the person is seen as selfish and uncaring, or they are seen as excited and understandably distracted...which one feels better for you? If you can choose the story—one that also leaves you feeling better, why wouldn't you?

When working on cognitions with my clients, they may challenge me by asking if I want them to change the thought to something they do not believe. I usually request that they try to find something more general, which they are open to believing, even if they are not 100% convinced. As a rule, it's easier to accept new ways of seeing things when we can "buy into it" more fully. To begin, one must first let go of the negative thought that is not serving them, by "poking holes" in it, or discrediting it from being 100% true. Once they can do this, they can more easily begin to entertain the idea that other possibilities might be true.

Invitation: Challenge Your Thoughts

An example of challenging a cognition could be altering an idea such as, "The world is filled with horrible, selfish people." If I carry this belief around, I will almost exclusively pay attention to any evidence that supports my hypothesis. Let's face it, we all like to feel that we are right. However, the opposite is also true; if I believe the world is predominantly filled with good people, doing the best they can to treat others with love and respect, I will unconsciously seek confirmation of this belief. In the beginning of exchanging one belief for another, I would ask that you find some evidence to discredit the initial negative belief (to find any support you can that not everyone is selfish). All we need to do is begin to "poke holes" in our belief. For example, recalling a time someone was kind and considerate would discredit the idea that "everyone" is horrible and selfish. From there, one can begin to find a reasonable opposing statement, such as "the world is predominantly filled with good people doing the best they can to treat others with love and respect." This statement only asserts that "most" people (leaving wiggle room) are "doing the best they can" (which leaves more room for human mistakes and imperfection). This is a subtle way to begin to drop the resistance to changing our beliefs.

One way you could implement this with your estranged spouse would be switching your view of their undesirable behavior as being an intentional act designed to harm you to instead seeing it as a result of their inability to recognize how harmful or hurtful it is to you. Or, if this is not possible, imagine instead how sad it is that they are not able to make more kind or loving choices at this time due to whatever they are struggling with internally. Again, this is not about condoning their behavior, but rather choosing not to be held mentally captive by it.

Invitation: Rearrange Those Thoughts

Redirecting your thoughts may be very hard at first. But when you consider the positive experiences you gained through your marital union (like friendships, travel, financial stability, knowledge, self-awareness, boundary awareness, clarification of needs, or children), you can certainly find at least one positive takeaway from your marriage to think about. Another option is to use reframing, the psychotherapeutic technique in which you look at the same situation from a different angle, or even find the silver lining to your current experience of transition (however difficult it may be to find).

The positive aspect you choose to focus upon is not meant to outweigh the negatives. In fact, it may seem insignificant compared to the upsetting experience of your dissolved/dissolving relationship. Whether or not your perspective shifts permanently is not important. Choosing to place your attention on a positive aspect, even if only for a moment, will allow you to feel a physical shift in your body. You will then be able to release unproductive negative emotions, because you have taken your attention away from them.

Removing our attention from the emotional energy we experience (after we have acknowledged it) allows that energy to do what energy does—move on. With persistent life issues, like divorce, we can expect the emotional energy to return at some point, but building our skills to release it when we need some relief is a tremendous asset to our wellbeing.

This is an exercise to practice each and every day. When anger or other disruptive thoughts related to your partner arise, shift your perspective of the situation to focus on another aspect or angle.

You might consider finding thoughts of gratitude or lovingkindness. Recall that lovingkindness is a feeling of tenderness, friendliness, and consideration. Keep in mind it may not be easy to switch gears from an upset feeling to a pleasant one. But the point is to try, to think the thoughts or even say the words out loud if that helps. You can find the positive aspect of a situation in the midst of your negative experience. Both positive and negative thoughts are available to you in this moment and at all times. It only depends where you choose to look.

Chapter 21 Tools:

• Decide to create a different life perspective and watch your emotions shift. Becoming more aware of your thoughts and self-talk will allow you to work with the unproductive and unhealthy thoughts you discover.

• Notice and write down in the space provided some specific instances when it is more difficult for you to work with your thoughts. Perhaps there are specific situations in which you struggle to consider an alternate way of viewing things. For now, just take note of the areas in which you struggle, and trust that you can come back to them at a later time.

_____

_____

_____

_____

_____

_____

_____

_____

Chapter 22

Evolving Your Emotions

*"Your intellect may be confused, but your
emotions will never lie to you."*

– Roger Ebert

Taking an Honest Look: Self-Awareness

During intense turning points, like divorce, people
question and examine their lives. Why must we experience
life's challenges? What is the point of falling in and out of
love? When we go through situations in life that we deem
unpleasant, we may find it difficult to understand the
reason for the experience. The truth is, even if we hold a
spiritual belief that all things work for the best, we still
might question the specific purpose or express
disappointment with our higher power for the tremendous
heartache. On a base level, I do believe we are given these
events in life to teach us lessons to promote our further
growth and evolution. If you share this perspective, it
provides additional support for moving through your
divorce with kindness and faith for an ultimately positive
outcome—*for all parties involved.* Further, it suggests that
it is important to pause at crucial moments to examine
what lesson is being offered to us.

Every relationship requires two participants to create a
relational dynamic. Taking some time to explore what you

contributed to the dynamic is a way to keep yourself "in check" and out of a blame game with your partner. Even if you believe your negative contribution was significantly less than that of your partner, you can still gain insight. Often, particularly during times of stress, we behave in ways that seem quite reasonable to us. Most likely, these behaviors were a creative adaptation to our environment in childhood. At some point, these behaviors likely became a pattern of response we engaged in without considering how it contributed to the negative response we received from others. Only by taking personal inventory can you hope to engage in new ways and find different results in relationships. Whether you stay in or leave your marriage, your personal insights will benefit you for the rest of your life.

How We Co-Create Our Relationships: Marcus's Story

Marcus had been separated from his wife of two years when he came for therapy. He described feeling "smothered" and perceived his wife as critical and controlling. Marcus was an avid golfer, playing on Saturday and Sunday most weekends. He shared that when he did not play golf, he was watching sports with his friends at the local sports bar. Marcus had a stressful job and reported these hobbies brought him a great deal of stress relief.

When questioned, Marcus shared that his wife did not play golf with him and "isn't invited." He laughed. Upon further exploration, Marcus shared that his wife criticized him for "not caring" about her, and she often "whined and cried" that she felt lonely in their marriage. With a great deal of frustration, Marcus reported that this dynamic had been a pattern in his past relationships as well. "When she acts like that, why would I want to come home at all?! I'm a grown man; I won't be held captive!" Just prior to moving out, Marcus had been spending even more time out of the house, working late at the office and eating out with friends.

Therapeutically, it was suggested that Marcus might be contributing to the criticism and "nagging" he was receiving from his wife, as well as the experience that his wife was attempting to "control" him. Marcus had not considered that he might not be investing adequate time and attention to sustain his marriage. He began to consider that his wife might be ineffectively asking for something reasonable, rather than merely intending to shame and control him. Certainly, she had her own marital contributions to address. However, Marcus's ability to see that his wife might not be "so awful" and might not actually wish to control him were helpful in allowing him to see his personal patterns of avoidance, outside of his wife's behavior.

<u>Finding Your Patterns</u>

Exploring your relational dynamics can be much more difficult than it may sound. This is in part because it is far easier to see the faults we perceive in someone else than to be fully aware of our own actions and how they are perceived and impact others. It is important to remember that the world is our mirror. The dynamics you co-created in your marriage are just that, co-created. I am not suggesting that every relational dynamic is 50/50. Sometimes, the division of responsibility for unhealthy behavior is 60/40 or even 80/20. But we all have choices, and we only allow from others what fits or is working for us (in some way or another). It may be that your relationship dynamic worked for you at the time you agreed to enter that relationship. But as you continued to grow, the dynamic between you no longer fit. An example of this is a stereotypical codependent dynamic in which one person sacrifices their needs to act as a caregiver for the other person's needs. If one person decides to mature in self-care, begins to implement boundaries, and refuses to interact in the same manner, the relationship dynamic will be strained.

The idea that we allow into our life what makes sense to us or works for us can be hard to believe. Especially if you found yourself in an abusive or emotionally damaging relationship. However, taking an honest look to understand where you failed to honor yourself, your boundaries, your values, or your needs is the first step.

Often, our own diminished sense of self-worth, unresolved issues from the past, and the codependent process cause us to make conscious and unconscious choices that ultimately do not serve us. Learning about, and most importantly, taking responsibility for our own contributions empowers us to make different, healthier choices, and heal our wounds.

If it is unclear what you contributed, this would be a wonderful time to begin exploring more deeply by reading books, asking trusted friends for their opinions of what they saw from the outside, consulting with your ex-partner (if this can be done safely and kindly), or talking with a professional. Reading books, attending workshops, or participating in support groups can also facilitate healing and insight. Reading suggestions can be found in the back of the book, as considerations to further support your evolution.

Working on Your Patterns

Once you have determined what your unhealthy patterns are, you will want to examine the emotions that are driving your behavior, or the emotions you are avoiding by engaging in said behavior. Emotional repair work begins with a decided commitment to first being present with your emotions. Engaging in mindful awareness and the act of accepting your emotions as they arise is important to being able to move through and "process" emotions. It is equally important to know when to dive more deeply into exploring emotions—when to simply notice them, acknowledge them, and release them. A therapist is extremely helpful in looking from the outside at what plagues your mind and assisting you in using your brain power productively. Left to the devices of our untrained minds, our mental focus can feel drawn to our thoughts like a magnet to 1980s refrigerator, regardless of whether it is purposeful for us or not.

When I first suggest the idea of "noticing and releasing" emotions to clients, they usually respond in disbelief. It can feel like big emotions are entirely hijacking our minds, and the idea of simply *releasing* emotionally powerful or enticing thoughts may sound impossible. But, if you recall from Section II, an emotion only takes ninety seconds to move through our body. So, if we let go of the sustaining belief or troubling thought and focus only on the physical manifestation of the emotion, we can train our minds to do exactly this—let go.

Another way of thinking about it is to stand squarely in front of our emotion and allow it to be completely what it is, which is the basis of Gestaltist Fritz Perls' *Paradoxical Theory of Change*. In fact, facing our emotion head on can lead us to deeper realizations that will facilitate emotional healing. This paradoxical theory allows us the freedom to let go of troubling emotional experiences through the ironic process of accepting the experience exactly as it is occurring within us in the moment. So often we attempt to get rid of our internal emotional experience by denying it, pushing it away, or focusing on it in an attempt to solve it. Ironically, fully letting ourselves feel our experience allows the energy of that experience to move on. In other words, we "honor" it, by acknowledging it as our experience, then we allow it to move on as we focus on other things (preferably positive things that bring us joy). Esther Hicks, an inspirational speaker and author on the law of attraction, would say the more you resist something, the more you attention you give it, the more of it you will see it in your life. And let's be honest, none of us want more negative feelings!

When we practice this, in the midst of our emotional experience and afterward, we are able to recognize and accept some powerful insights—all because we stopped resisting our true experience. A similar practice is popularized in Buddhist psychology and exemplified in mindfulness meditation. Aimed at the goal of releasing emotions (not necessarily to process them), this aspect of practicing non-attachment helps us stop feeling controlled by our internal experiences. In this practice, the practitioner also feels the experience, noticing and acknowledging it, but then allows it to leave as easily as it came. It is not necessary to determine ahead of time whether you need to process deeper awareness of an emotion or just let it go entirely. In my personal and professional experience, the very act of letting go starts to allow for the needed realizations to come forward into our awareness as we are ready to receive them.

Emotional healing during your divorce can be best supported and expedited by consulting with a therapist. In addition to therapy, activities like journaling provide a wonderful way to process the experiences we need to further examine, especially those that we are not ready to discuss with others. Occasionally, and if you're both open and willing, there may also be opportunities to process your emotions with your estranged marital partner. When this is the case, it is important to set clear boundaries with yourself and your partner about what is relevant to share. While this can be tremendously beneficial for you both, you must keep in mind that it's not necessary to relay everything you think and feel to your ex-partner. Without clear parameters and a commitment to keep the conversation productive and kind, this type of interaction could easily go off the rails and lead to additional hurt and negativity between you both. Again, a couples therapist can provide tremendous help here by keeping your conversations productive.

Supporting Yourself Daily

As I discussed in Section II, it is very important to take care of yourself. DAILY. Each day, you need a plan for the things you will do to keep yourself in the healthiest emotional space possible—feeling as good as you can so you can better handle the heavy stuff in the divorce. Research supports that while medication can mask the symptoms and thus support a sense of well-being, and therapy can begin to work on the issues that require change, the best foundational approach to mental health management is "The Big Three" outlined in Section II. Eat breakfast every day, exercise at least thirty minutes per day, and sleep seven to nine hours every night. Remember to develop your daily/weekly rituals and to check in with what you need, even if you can't meet that need to the fullest in the moment—try to give yourself some approximation of that need (just like grabbing a snack when you're starving). For more assistance with this, see the Self-Care Planning Guide from page 96.

Remember that it is not realistic to expect yourself to exist without feeling negative emotions during your separation or divorce. Perhaps, you'll experience *very strong* negative emotions. To make matters worse, you may have conflicting emotions that seem to turn on a dime. This is why it is imperative that you commit to a self-care routine. You must build resilience to tolerate the roller coaster of emotions inherent in the divorce process. It is important to remember that if you do not create your personal plan for self-care and commit to it, you are unlikely to engage in it during the moments you need it most!

Understanding Self-Care

You can think of self-care behavior with a two-fold application: an ongoing preventative approach and a practical application used during crucial life moments.

To better understand the preventative approach, I like to use the analogy of a pot of water on a stove. When you place a cool pot of water on the stove, you can turn the dial all the way to 10, and it will still take a significant amount of time for the pot to become so hot it boils over. But if you leave a pot simmering at a level 7 or 8, turning that pot up to 10 will cause it to boil in a matter of moments. The stress that is inherent in the divorce process means that you may likely be unavoidably hovering at a minimum of level 3-4 at any given time. Your goal is to engage in activities that keep your stress level no higher than a level 6.

You must leave room for unexpected stressors and triggers, lest you boil over each time you are surprised or hurt by a poorly timed comment or from your estranged partner, their attorney, your children, or family or friends.

The crucial application of self-care is like treating a physical wound. You do not need antibacterial wash, salve, and a bandage most days, but if you fall and skin your elbow, you definitely want to be ready with the appropriate treatment. You should have a list with ideas of things to do when you're feeling especially low, stressed, angry, or anxious. You know yourself better than anyone, so think of things that lift your spirits, bring you peace, or leave you feeling more centered. If you struggle to think of things, ask a close friend or family member for some help.

Chapter 22 Tools:

• Once you're paying greater attention in your life, you will likely discover patterns in your behavior that you did not previously see. Only when we see our patterns can we learn to make new choices and engage in behaviors that will better serve us. This is a wonderful time to consider therapy or self-help books, while your access to recent patterns is fresh and readily available.

• Utilize the Paradoxical Theory of Change by standing squarely in your emotions and owning them, even if you do not like what you are experiencing. Once you have let go of the thought and focus on the emotion, you can allow the experience to move on its way.

· Support yourself daily with self-care behaviors. Make a list below of things that are supportive and recharging for you. Find ways to implement these, not just when you're feeling low, but every single day. A list can be found on page 99 to assist you in determining what will work best.

_____

_____

_____

_____

_____

_____

_____

_____

Chapter 23

Clarifying Your Relational Goals...
and How You Interrupt Them

"Setting goals is the first step in turning the invisible into the visible."

– Tony Robbins

Detachment: Letting Go with Love

At some point, there will be a time when you are emotionally ready to let go of the past and your ties to your relationship as it was so that you may move forward. This may come with your decision to file for divorce, or as you approach the legal end of your marriage. Your decision to let go of the past will help facilitate your grieving process, a necessary part of endings. Loss of something once valued results in grief. Even if you do not like your spouse at the present moment, you, at one time, valued the idea of marriage with this person in some capacity. Letting go of your dream or hope for the future has its own grief, which may be separate from the grief of letting go of your ex-partner. Additionally, you may grieve the loss of your family unit, the loss of a friendship, sexual partner, source of physical affection, travel companion, co-parenting partner, financial partner, dinner companion, or sharer of life goals. Keep in mind that new life routines, losing social contacts, changing automobiles and residences, and letting go of shared possessions can also elicit feelings of grief. Despite your willingness to let go, there were certainly parts of your marriage that worked well or that you enjoyed, and it is healthy and reasonable for you to miss those parts, even if you are ready to let go of your marriage.

Grieving toward Acceptance

Various aspects of change in your life may carry separate grief experiences, and it is important to recognize and honor your experience in each step. The process of letting go of your relationship can be facilitated by finding closure. One way to do this is to perform a ceremony, with or without your partner, to honor the relationship. At the close of this chapter, you will find ideas for letting go ceremonies you can do alone or ideally with your ex to assist with relationship closure.

As mentioned above, we may grieve different aspects of our relationship at various and unexpected times. Each stage of grief allows a new opportunity to release our partner through forgiveness. I will touch briefly on the stages of grief, as understanding where we are in our emotional process can facilitate acceptance and forward movement. Made very popular by Elisabeth Kübler-Ross (1997), the five stages of grief include denial, anger, bargaining, depression, and acceptance. Clients often ask me to identify their stage, under the assumption that they are predictable and operate in this checklist order. While it would be wonderful if life and emotions were that predictable, these stages come in differing or overlapping order, skipping around and repeating themselves. They do, however, offer a general framework for understanding what is reasonable during the grief process, which can normalize what you might be experiencing. Some stages can last quite a long time, and others move more quickly, while some repeat themselves several times over. I have also witnessed clients who arrive for their first therapy session having been stuck in one stage for years due to a need for deeper work in the area of unresolved trauma and childhood family dynamics. For this reason, it is important to attend to your grief and practice emotional work, like the ones suggested in this book, to allow the grief process to unfold. If you find you are lingering in unnecessary suffering, please seek additional support.

Often in divorce, the grieving process has already begun from within the still intact marriage. Some marital partners grieve the loss of their sexual partner or best friend early in the marriage and move through the stages of grief long before exiting the marriage. Some may believe they have fully grieved their marriage by the time they file divorce paperwork. In my professional experience, it has never completely been the case. This does not mean we must go through our grief for a predetermined amount of time, nor that everyone needs therapy to grieve, but until we do our emotional work and are able to let go and forgive, it is difficult to release the energy of grief.

In summary, regardless of how happy you may feel to let go of an unhealthy marriage, there is still some amount of grief that will follow the completion of your divorce. In other words, grief is unpredictable but is also necessary and manageable. Do not attempt to ignore or rigidly control your grieving process. Allow your grief to unfold, and accept yourself wherever you are. You can use the skills discussed in this book, including mindfulness, acceptance, and the ninety-second rule, to help you along. You will want to reflect on your grief enough to facilitate the process as it moves along, rather than trying to speed it up or becoming stuck by fixating on or "burying" parts of it.

Closing Out Your Relationship Chapter

Ending a marriage, however difficult and disappointing it may have been, is a painful and emotionally heavy experience. I have often seen clients deliberately "block off" difficult feelings and focus only on the relief of being "done" with their tumultuous marriage. While this is also a natural desire during divorce, focusing only on the finalization aspect delays processing your grief—which has a funny way of showing up in your next relationship as significant fear or anger. Additionally, you may find yourself in an exaggerated response of grief or depression following the end of a brief dating relationship if you do not fully experience the grief of your current relationship's end.

I have found that as relationally based individuals, we are better able to move on from our painful past when we have a "coherent narrative" of that experience. Dan Siegel, a UCLA neuropsychiatrist, has written at length on this topic. He shares ideas about the importance of "making sense" of our life story to cultivate "strength and resilience" (Siegel, 2010). Siegel discusses what I and countless other therapists have experienced in the midst of our work: it is crucial to be present in both positive and negative experiences and be able to weave them together into the story of our lives. In honoring our journey, it is important to be fully present with our experience in each moment, including the termination of important relationships.

Research supports what I have personally and professionally experienced, which is this: creating a ceremony to honor the act of emotionally letting go can facilitate processing our emotional grief. Basically, the more ways you can support your emotional processing, the better. Reflecting honesty on your experience allows you to assimilate the lessons you have learned and create your coherent narrative to support your "emotional integration," becoming fully immersed within an experience. Developing a healthy, coherent, integrated narrative of our difficult life experiences is a fundamental aspect of our emotional health. Again, a therapist is a wonderful resource to assist you in navigating the sometimes-confusing process of moving through grief. But with or without a therapist, grief is not something that will be ignored. Thus, addressing it with intention is our best approach. As we gain closure of past relational struggles, we leave ourselves in a healthier place from which we can more confidently embark on our journey ahead. An example of a letting go ceremony can be found on the next page.

Therapeutic Invitation:

Before concluding, take one last moment to reevaluate your post-divorce vision. Notice anything that has changed and readjust your vision. As you move forward in your contemplation or divorce process, periodically, revisit this vision and renew your commitment to it. Remember that in doing so, you are renewing your commitment to your most positive and peaceful future. And we must first envision that something is possible to achieve it.

Chapter 23 Tools:

- There are many aspects of your relationship that you may grieve, even if you are "happy" to be ending your marriage. Leave space for yourself to grieve however you need to. Be aware that grief may show up in different ways at unpredictable times. Be gentle with yourself.

- Allow yourself to have a full and "coherent narrative" of your marital life. Keep in mind it wasn't *all bad,* even though you may feel that way now. Try to remember your journey in a manner that honors the whole experience. If it helps, you can use the space below to recall some positive aspects of your relationship. Holding a more balanced view of your marriage will help you move forward in your life in a healthier way.

_____

_____

_____

_____

_____

_____

_____

_____

Letting Go Ceremony: Steps to Healing

The letting go ceremony is a unique exercise that may be performed individually, but ideally by the couple, if both parties are willing to do so openly. It is certainly not for everyone, but the ceremony can be a powerful tool for closure as you end your relationship. The letting go ceremony is a gesture that honors the good times as well as the bad (as these are often times of growth and reflection). There are many ways this can be performed, and while I have outlined what I did, but please be creative in selecting the most meaningful ceremony for your relationship.

During our marriage, my ex and I honeymooned in Thailand and released a Thai lantern into the sky above the ocean on one memorable night. To honor this, we elected to release a Thai lantern over the lake near our home for our letting go ceremony as well. We wrote our best memories and positive wishes for each other on the lantern and attempted to send it off above the lake. Unfortunately, the lantern would not take flight—which became quite amusing to me, symbolically speaking. We then decided to burn the lantern...only to find the paper was flame retardant and would not hold the flame!

So, determined and stubborn as we both are, we slowly burnt little sections, one at a time, until the lantern was ash.

It did not go as we had pictured it in our heads—much like our marriage—but in this case, we were able to have a good laugh and make the best of the situation. One thing we always did well was laugh together.

Burning mementos can be a cathartic experience, as can burying something, meditating on a focused theme, reading a piece of poetry, or creating a piece of art together. The important thing is honoring the experience of the relationship, filled with both easy times and hard times.

Again, this is not for everyone. But if you have one small part of you that is open to the idea, I would highly recommend proposing the idea to your partner. You may get more out of it than you imagine.

Section V

Practices & Exercises

*"Anger is an acid that can do more harm to
the vessel in which it is stored than to
anything in which is it poured."*
—Mark Twain

In many of the exercises below, it will be suggested that you focus on your breath. The use of breath is an important aspect of these exercises for a variety of reasons. Breath helps you calm your nervous system to assist you with processing the emotional content in some of the activities offered below. Additionally, our breath is our life force and is one way that we center into ourselves. From this centered place, we are better equipped to access our highest self and truest nature, and thus, we are more likely to function from a place of love.

COGNITIVE & EMOTIONAL EXERCISES

While we cannot control our automatic thoughts, we can choose which thoughts we hold on to for longer periods of time and which we let go more quickly. Recall that your emotions are the direct result of what you spend your time thinking about. If a thought leaves you feeling badly and doesn't serve a productive purpose, let it leave your mind, and your emotions will soon follow. The following exercises will help you examine and work differently with your thoughts, or *cognitions*.

These cognitive exercises can be done at anytime, anywhere—and I will encourage you to practice them that way! In the beginning, it may help to do them on a daily basis to increase your practice using them. The emotional work exercises below will support you in processing the heavy emotions that accompany divorce so they may be released. Keep in mind that this is a process; the key to healing and growth is to continue to work at it even in the moments when you'd rather burrow down into your righteous anger or depression.

EXERCISE 1—Rearrange Those Thoughts

Redirecting your thoughts may be very hard at first. But when you consider the positive experiences you gained through your marital union (like friendships, travel, financial stability, knowledge, self-awareness, boundary awareness, clarification of needs, or children), you can certainly find *at least one* positive takeaway from your marriage to think about. Another option is to use reframing, the psychotherapeutic technique in which you look at the same situation from a different angle, or even find the silver lining to your current experience of transition (however difficult it may be to find). The positive aspect you choose to focus upon is not meant to outweigh the negatives. In fact, it may seem insignificant compared to the upset from your dissolved/dissolving relationship. Whether or not your perspective shifts permanently is not important. Choosing to place your attention on a positive aspect, even if only for a moment, will allow you to feel differently in your body and give you space to release any unproductive emotions, by taking your focus off of them. Removing our attention from the emotional energy we experience (after we have acknowledged it) allows that energy to do what energy does—move on. With ongoing life issues, like divorce, we can expect the emotional energy to return at some point, but building our skills to release it when we need some relief is a tremendous asset to our wellbeing.

This is an exercise to practice each and every day. When anger or other disruptive thoughts related to your partner arise, shift your perspective of the situation and focus on another aspect or from a different angle. You might consider thinking thoughts of gratitude or lovingkindness. Recall that lovingkindness is a feeling of tenderness, friendliness, and consideration. Keep in mind it may not be easy to switch gears from an upset feeling to a pleasant one. But the point is to *try*, to think the thoughts or even say the words out loud if that helps. You can find the positive aspect of a situation in the midst of your negative experience. Both positive and negative thoughts are available to you in this moment and at all times. It only depends where you choose to look.

EXERCISE 2—Shift Your Thinking

Stop trying to solve the problem of your emotions or the ways you would like your partner to change, particularly, if you have decided to let go of the relationship. Instead, focus on accepting *what is,* rather than continuing to lament what you wish had been. There is tremendous suffering to bear when we choose to "wallow" in our disappointment. It is important to have enough compassion for ourselves that we stop fixating on things we cannot control and shift our focus elsewhere entirely. Practicing *mindfulness* can assist with conditioning your brain to redirect to thoughts that serve you better in the moment. *Meditation* can also be an effective "distraction" from your pain. Keep in mind that attempting to meditate in a particularly heightened state of emotional arousal is not an effective strategy. You must build a practice during moments that are free from intense distress. This is how a meditation practice is helpful—you build the skill that you can then more easily call upon it during difficult moments. The key to effective application of cognitive redirection is *making a choice* to move your thoughts to something else,

REBECCA HARVEY, PSY. D.

rather than wasting time and emotions spinning in upsetting, unproductive thoughts.

For your practice, bring to mind a time when you felt completely relaxed and happy. Notice where you were, what you were doing, and what was going on around you. Spend some time focusing on the details of the experience. Notice how you feel in your body to really enrich the experience. Now bring a thought to mind of something that recently was irritating or upsetting with your ex or about your divorce. It might help to start with something relatively small to illustrate this exercise, like a level 2–3 rating situation on a scale of 10, with 10 being most disturbing. You can always practice with bigger things once you feel more comfortable with the exercise. Now notice yourself thinking about the upsetting thought and make the choice to *stop* and switch over to the positive experience you just had in your mind. Stay with that positive experience until you feel your emotions and body sensations begin to shift back into a positive state. If you'd like, you can move back and forth between the two thoughts, noting how your emotional experience changes. You may notice that it is easier to get "sucked in" by your negative thoughts. This is natural but can interrupt your effort to stay in a positive emotional space. Recognize you have the ability to switch between these thoughts by exerting your mental power. This reminds you that you do not have to stay spinning in your negative thought patterns but can redirect to different thoughts when it is beneficial for you.

EXERCISE 3—Challenging Your Cognitions

Often, we accept our thoughts and perceive them as facts. From this place, we may feel righteous, or justified anger about a situation. To be clear, your thoughts are not facts. They are the opinions and experiences you have woven together to give you a shortcut to understanding the way the world operates. This is why people have such dramatically different beliefs and perspectives from one another. We can change our present emotional upset by asking ourselves a very simple question, "Is my thought on this a guaranteed fact with no other possible perspective if seen by a different person?" This does not mean "would your friends or neighbors share your opinion?" Rather, would this, *from every other possible perspective,* be seen exactly as you see it now? Is it provable, undeniable, and written in stone?

Chances are, even if the situation could be seen as a fact in the operational details, it would not be seen as fact in an emotional interpretation of the situation. For example, you would understand your ex's motivation behind their "bad" behavior differently than a neutral person (like the grocery store clerk) or your ex's friends or family. When we suspend judgement and stop operating as if we know all of the answers, we may begin to soften our hard-lined stance of holding "the ultimate truth" above our partner's truth.

This expanded awareness can reduce our experience of righteous anger.

Working with your cognitions by challenging them allows you the option of softening your stance and allowing space for a difference of opinion or experience. When we can do this, we are more likely to release our grip on our anger, contempt, resentment, and even hurt feelings.

<u>EXERCISE 4—Paradoxical Release of Anger</u>

Just like all other emotions, anger is an appropriate emotion. Much of the time, anger is informing us about a boundary. Sometimes, we are angry because others have violated our boundary, and sometimes, we are angry because we have violated our own boundary by doing something we did not want to do. We usually do this to avoid another undesirable emotion, like guilt, hurt, or sadness. Anger itself is not bad. The way we choose to express our anger however, can be. We can learn to let go of anger.

In this exercise, close your eyes and allow something that angers you to come to mind. Start slowly, with something that rates at a 3 or 4 on a scale of 0–10, with 10 being most upsetting. As you bring this feeling to mind, notice where you feel it in your body (i.e., jaw, stomach, fists). Next, imagine what color it might be, as well as what shape, size, and texture. Brining this image to mind will help you hold your focus on the sensation of the emotion. Allow yourself permission to feel your anger, without guilt, and do not analyze it as reasonable or unreasonable, for it does not matter—focus only on the feelings. Now say to yourself, "This is anger," or "I feel angry when I think about ____." Notice that it is possible to just *feel* your anger and not respond in an inappropriate manner.

Honor your experience of anger and practice having reasonable conversations with yourself, expressing your feelings without blame or defensiveness. For example, you may say, "I feel angry because I expected _____, and instead, I got ____." Or, "I feel very angry because I did not want to do _____, and I allowed myself to agree to it anyway." Or, "I feel furious because I told them not to do _____, and yet they did it anyhow."

After you have worked through a conversation or two in your mind, notice again the areas in your body where your anger resides. Identify the color, shape, and texture of the feeling, and try to remain with the visual awareness for the next couple of minutes. You should notice the feeling subsiding within a couple of minutes if you can refrain from going back to the upsetting thought (recall the ninety-second rule). From this more relaxed place you can either distract yourself to another subject entirely or move on to cognitive interventions (from other exercises in this book) to work with your experience on a deeper level.

You can apply this same exercise to foster acceptance of any difficult feelings you are trying to work though.

Remember not to judge what you find, but just notice and allow yourself space to create self-understanding. For example, "This is guilt (or sadness); I feel guilty (or sad) when I consider_____. I feel guilty (or sad) because _____."

EXERCISE 5—Not Mine

Sometimes, we get pulled into other people's emotions. This is especially true for highly sensitive people, or *empaths*. It is important to recognize when you are being pulled into someone else's emotions and learn to create an emotional boundary to separate their feelings from your own. We all have the right to our feelings, and as long as we are not being abusive or intrusive to others, we have the right to feel our feelings as we see fit. Allow others the space to feel their feelings and yourself the space not to join them. Sometimes, other people will want you to be in their emotion with them (or for them) and may be upset when you decline the invitation to join them. This is okay. They may fuss or throw a tantrum and that is also okay. You do not need to respond to other's dissatisfaction in those moments.

When you feel yourself being pulled into someone else's emotional experience or find yourself thinking negatively about someone, I suggest one of two options. I have come across versions of this from various books and energy healers. The idea is to disconnect your energy from the other person's energy. The first option is simply saying out loud, "This is not mine. Get out!" and imagine physically taking the emotion from your body and tossing it out. This is a great way to manage rumination on any unproductive negative emotion that exhausts your time and energy resources.

However, my favorite version of this exercise is a gentler approach that leaves me feeling better inside. I imagine the emotion, take a deep breath into the space I feel it in my body, and then imagine breathing it out as I send it back to the other person, saying, "I send this back to you with consciousness and love." The result of this last practice leaves me feeling peaceful and loving. The truth is, if the feeling is not mine, there is nothing for me to do with it, and the other person needs to deal with it on their own.

EXERCISE 6—Cultivating Courage

Fear is one of the most limiting emotions we can experience. While it is true that bad things can happen, we tend to exaggerate the unknown negative outcomes we fear. I love the ideas in Susan Jeffers' book *Feel the Fear and Do It Anyway*. When you're in a state of fear, she suggests, examine the worst possible outcome and coach yourself through the reality that you would be able to handle it (even if you would hate for it to happen). By doing this, you can feel your fear about the unknown outcomes of various situations, but move forward despite the fear. In a situation like divorce, you will often be forced to move forward despite your fear caused by your partner or the legal process.

In this exercise, you are asked to sit quietly with just one idea of something that is fearfully upsetting to you. As you hold this idea in your mind, take a deep breath into your belly and slowly let it out. Begin to repeat to yourself, "It is okay for me to feel frightened sometimes. I can handle difficult situations with ease. I am okay now. I will be okay then. This experience and this fear is temporary. I can trust myself to take care of myself and seek help when I need it." Then take another deep breath and let it all the way out. Imagine giving yourself a big hug. You've got this.

EXERCISE 7—Fostering Vulnerability

It is through vulnerability that we find true strength and freedom, for in vulnerability, we are in our authentic self. Showing up as your authentic self leaves you with a sense of integrity in all that you do. Even when things do not go your way, you can rest in the knowledge that you were true to yourself in each moment. Retaining our vulnerable strength is difficult at times, particularly in situations you may encounter during your separation or divorce. Being able to speak to your partner from a place of truth, without blaming, shaming, or making yourself a victim, will assist you in finding your inner freedom and supporting your healthiest process.

In this meditation exercise, find a quiet place to sit or lay down. Take 3–10 full, deep breaths and let your body relax. Once you have found a quiet space within, begin to repeat the following statements, along with any other statements that feel are supportive and true to you in cultivating your vulnerability:

"I accept myself fully, exactly as I am."

"I am open to feeling whatever emotions arise."

"I release any feelings of shame—I am good."

"It is okay for me to have any feelings I experience."

"I am safe and secure. I am not my emotions."

"I am enough. I am whole. I am worthy. I am lovable."

"I can speak my truth, even when it feels difficult."

"I do not need others' approval of my emotions."

"I can keep myself safe."

Repeat three or more times any phrases that feel true and resonate with you. Perhaps, try a few phrases that you would like to believe, but might not just yet. Continue breathing and notice how you feel in your body as you move through this exercise and for a few minutes afterward.

EXERCISE 8—Retaining Respect

This exercise is designed to help you consider what behaviors will support your best efforts to be respectful of yourself and your partner. Before important conversations, phone calls, or meetings, review this list. Use it as a gentle reminder in order to support your post-divorce vision.

• Try to listen with curiosity, rather than preparing your response in your own mind while your ex is speaking.

• Try to find some validity in your partner's response prior to sharing your point of view.

• Be aware of your facial expressions and body language. Try to keep them pleasant or neutral.

• Be aware that your tone is kind and calm. Avoid condescending, annoyed, or otherwise rude tones.

• When you disagree, explain your position with "I" statements. Remember, your position is based on your opinion, your perspective, and your feelings...not a universal rule of how the whole world perceives things.

• Get comfortable with saying you're sorry when you have made a mistake or not been your best self.

• Speak to your partner as though they are intelligent (even if you do not believe they are).

• Consider compassion when trying to understand your ex. Try to remove them from the "calculating villain" role. Most people are not planning to intentionally cause you pain and suffering.

• Refrain from criticizing, blaming, and shaming. Phrase your statements in regards to what is important to you rather than what they are not getting right.

EXERCISE 9—Cutting the Cord

I credit this exercise to an energy healer from Hawaii named Hannah Taua. The point of the exercise is to disconnect your energetic or emotional ties to another person. It is designed to reduce the emotional impact they have on you and to reduce your upset in situations involving them. Hannah instructs that this exercise be done three times, once per day over three consecutive days and then repeated once a week for the next four weeks.

As she instructs, first you visualize a cord running from your belly button to your ex-partner's or the situation you are trying to disconnect from. If you cannot visualize it, you can say out loud, "I see a cord running from my belly button to [your ex's name]." You can also include any other people or situations with which you are struggling. You then imagine grabbing that cord and "dramatically" pulling it out of your belly button while you say, "I'm pulling that cord off of me." Then dramatically throw it down and say, "In that hole, I place golden light," as you visualize placing a little ball of golden light into your belly button. Then tap your belly three times, and you're done.

I use this exercise as often as is necessary, when I feel a need to detach. I love this exercise because it offers something energetic, spiritual, and intentional to do with the lingering feelings and thoughts of your ex. It does not require you to never see them again or think poorly of them, but you are detaching your energy from theirs...with love.

EXERCISE 10—Acting As If

What would happen if...we imagined a struggle was already solved? Sometimes, we can become so preoccupied with an issue that we find it difficult to function effectively in other areas of life. In regards to emotional struggles, about which we have limited or no control, "acting as if" is an effective way to get through the day. To be clear, I am not suggesting you avoid realistic life matters, like caring for your children or paying your bills. But give yourself a break from difficulties that plague your mind, so that you can move your emotions into a more positive space and your energy into a more effective and productive mode.

For this exercise, draw a line through the middle of a piece of paper. On one side, write down the problem which troubles you. On the other side, write down a fantasized, realistic solution. Now close your eyes and imagine what it would feel like if this were truly the case. Notice how you feel in your body. Allow yourself to breathe in the relief, happiness, or peace your solution brings. Then exhale and decide it is so. Allow yourself to hold this image vividly in your mind for a few minutes before opening your eyes.

Let yourself begin working toward that goal by acting as though it is already the case. As Melody Beattie shares in *The Language of Letting Go,* "Acting as if is a positive way to overcome fear, doubts, and low self-esteem. We do not have to lie; we do not have to be dishonest with ourselves. We open up to the positive possibilities of the future, instead of limiting the future by today's feelings and circumstances" (Beattie, 1990). In most situations, we lack the direct control to force things to be as we wish. So why not imagine the best possible outcome? We will have to deal with the resulting outcome regardless of whether it goes as we hoped, but wasting time feeling the pain of it going badly robs us of today for a tomorrow that may never come.

EXERCISES FOCUSING ON FORGIVENESS

Prior to completing an exercise, check in to evaluate where you are mentally and emotionally. Create a scale in which you can rank your emotional experience with a 0 to 10 rating. In this case, 0 is no trace of negative feeling, and 10 is the most significant and overwhelming experience of negative feeling you can imagine. Prior to each forgiveness exercise, write down the number you are feeling, and after completing the exercise, write down the number associated with your current level of negative feeling. Do not be alarmed if occasionally your number does not move down or even goes up. Working through your emotions is a process, and sometimes, you will feel worse before you feel better.

EXERCISE 11—Storybook Release

Imagine yourself as a small child reading a colorful storybook. Picture yourself turning the pages. Imagine brightly colored illustrations depicting your life with your partner. Start from the beginning of your relationship when you first met. Run through your dating, engagement, and marriage. Be sure to notice some of the positive experiences as well as the negative. As you do this, notice the feelings that arise within you and just allow them to be what they are. If you feel happiness, smile or laugh. If you feel sadness or hurt, allow yourself to cry.

Now notice someone is sitting next to you and has been reading along in the same illustrated storybook. It is the child version of your ex-partner, and you realize they have been crying and smiling right along with you. Notice how it feels to share this experience and how you feel about them as you imagine them being impacted just as you are by these same shared life experiences. This may be hard, but try to stay with it. When you finish the exercise, notice how you feel about your ex-partner in the moment and whether your feelings have changed from when you first began. You may find a shift in your experience of them, even if only slightly. The truth is we are all sharing a human experience and doing our best in each moment. Try to keep in mind that your ex had hopes of things working out differently in their mind as well.

EXERCISE 12—Freedom through Forgiveness

1. On a large sheet of paper, take 10–25 minutes to list some of the hurts you have experienced from your ex. This list can be as exhaustive as you'd like, filled with small and large upsets. Once you have your list, break the hurts down into categories or themes (i.e., dishonesty, unkind words, control, neglect) and circle each category.

2. Sit in silence for 10–15 minutes and contemplate the motivation of your ex-partner's behavior. Dig deep here. Rather than creating them as a villain and you as a victim in your mind, stretch to see the fear, insecurity, hurt, shame, guilt, or ignorance behind their behavior. Consider for a moment their life experiences, trauma, childhood family background, and any mental illness or personality disorder they or their family may have had. Consider how your actions might have been received or interpreted by them in the absence of their ability to read your mind. Again, dig deep. This is just for you, and it is for your healing. You do not have to share your awareness with them or anyone else. Call upon the work you have been doing up to this point to increase your compassion, even if it is just a tiny amount. Give

whatever compassion you can. Once you have gained some insight and moved into a space of compassion for how they might have been feeling during the times they hurt you, you are then ready for the final step.

3. Say out loud:

_____, I forgive you for _____. I now have a deeper understanding of why you hurt me. I will no longer be hurt by you and will uphold my boundaries to take care of myself in a loving way. I am not condoning your behavior or making it okay, but I refuse to let it hold power over me any longer. I am free to release you and move forward in a healthy and happy way.

Repeat steps 2 and 3 of this exercise as often as necessary until you are able to genuinely wish your ex-partner well.

EXERCISE 13—Proclaiming Your Forgiveness

Imagine a scale of 0–10, with ten being most upset and 0 being not at all upset and determine how upset you are about a particular issue or with your ex in general. Next, while saying aloud "I forgive (your ex's name)," notice how this number shifts from higher to lower as you simply practice repeating the sentence while you sit with the idea of forgiving.

EXERCISE 14—Self-Forgiveness Mirror Work

This exercise can be very powerful and bring up some deep emotions if done in earnest. I find most mirror exercises to do the same. For this mirror exercise, you will need yourself and a mirror. It might be easiest to stand in front of a mirror, but you can use a hand mirror as well. You can best support this exercise by first making a list of the things about which you are upset with yourself (i.e., I did not hold my boundaries about our finances; I did not confront my partner's affairs, despite knowing about them; I knew this was not a healthy relationship and got married anyway; I didn't seek the support I needed and instead acted out in my marriage, etc.). Making a list helps you to focus on what runs through you mind and serves to keep you locked in your feelings of guilt and shame. However, you do not always need a list. You can do this exercise any time, on the fly, without a list.

For your practice, look into your eyes in the mirror and say, "I completely forgive myself for [insert upset here]," or "Even though I [insert something about which you are upset with yourself], I still love and accept myself." For example, "I completely forgive myself for acting out of anger today," or "Even though I lied to my spouse, I still love and accept myself." Repeat each sentence three times and then quietly look yourself in the eyes for several seconds as you notice what you feel. Let the truth of your experience sit with you and just notice.

You may find this difficult, or even hard to believe yourself. Do it anyway. You are not making your transgressions okay; you are freeing yourself from the binds of guilt and shame. In time, you will feel the benefits of this exercise, and you will find it easier to believe yourself and to truly forgive.

EXERCISE 15—Set Yourself Free

Because you are human, there are likely ways you have hurt or harmed your partner that create an opportunity for seeking forgiveness. Taking ownership over your own contributions is a powerful tool in the process of healing and obtaining closure. You may want to take some time to revisit (and possibly document) the timeline of your marriage, while taking an honest look at the places you did not shine your brightest. Write down some areas or incidents in which you could have been kinder, more supportive, more accepting, or more loving to your partner, and then decide if you would benefit from forgiving yourself alone, or from seeking forgiveness from your ex. If you do not have a safe or receptive ex, you can imagine or visualize a conversation in which you ask for their forgiveness and imagine them receiving your request with love and kindness.

EXERCISE 16—Revel in Revenge

I only suggest you engage in this if you are struggling to let go of your desire for your ex to suffer for their "crimes." Typically, it is best to move forward into a positive space where your ex and your emotions are concerned. But if you find yourself wanting bad things to happen to your ex-partner, allow yourself to momentarily own that feeling.

Let yourself fully embrace the fantasies you have for revenge, before you commit to letting go and moving on to forgiveness. Not everyone will feel a need to do this, but if you are currently in this negative emotional space, simply accept it as it is.

In this exercise, set a timer for 5–10 minutes. In that time, allow your mind to play out all of the "punishments" you believe your ex is due. You are only intended to do this exercise once, so decide what it is you need to get out of your system. When you have finished your designated time, set your fantasies aside and pick one of the other forgiveness exercises to complete. This last part is important—both to help you release your previous negative train of thought, and to move you into a different emotional space...and on toward the healing work of forgiveness.

SPIRITUAL EXERCISES

(Cultivating Compassion and Love)

Engaging in daily rituals of prayer, meditation, contemplation, or scriptural reading can provide peace of mind and increase faith and hope for the future. Use of spiritual practices can assist with letting go of unproductive cognitions and help you focus on positive and supportive thoughts.

EXERCISE 17—Blessing Circle

Imagine drawing a large circle and placing inside that circle everyone who carries emotion surrounding your divorce. This will obviously include your ex and yourself. You may also want to consider adding his or her attorney, family members, friends, the person with whom he or she was unfaithful (no, I'm not joking), or even your children if you have any divorce-related negative feelings. Anyone who has contributed or sustained emotions around your divorce can be placed in this circle—and the circle may change slightly from day to day (but will always include you and your partner).

Now the task becomes trickier. Your goal is to send blessings and forgiveness to each person, to include love, prosperity, peace, happiness, joy, success, wellbeing, understanding, compassion, and any other positive attribute you can imagine. You may notice resistance as you do this but keep with it! You can imagine sending these qualities from your heart in the form of light or brightly colored smoke, or my favorite option: liquid. Any liquid form you can imagine (water, paint, bubbles) from any source (rain, a bubble gun, a spray hose) will work. You should envision completely covering (or soaking) the person in light, smoke, or liquid, filled with happiness, blessings, and forgiveness. You will continue to focus on each individual until you see that person smiling back at you (I learned this last bit from a spiritual intuitive's visualization workshop and found that it was a true test of whether I had released negativity, if I could allow myself to see the person smiling back, so please don't skip this part). This exercise can be a difficult but powerful experience. But it will change the feeling in your body when you think of the previously upsetting individual. Do not forget to include yourself!

EXERCISE 18—Lovingkindness

One of the easiest ways to do a lovingkindness meditation is to imagine the person in your mind and repeat the words "lovingkindness." Lovingkindness meditation is a way to foster compassion for your ex. Not because they have earned it in any way, but simply because *they are, just as you are, a living soul.*

EXERCISE 19—Radical Gratitude

While it may seem impossible to think of the things you are grateful for about your ex, *it is possible*. The Bible says, "In all things be grateful." In Judaism, there are blessings to show gratitude for everything—the food we eat, the air we breathe, seeing a rainbow. Even mundane things are worthy of gratitude. A traditional Islamic saying states, "The first who will be summoned to paradise are those who have praised God in every circumstance."

For your practice, each morning (or night) write down three things about your life with your ex-partner that you are grateful for. Easy ones might be your children, learning to salsa dance, or for your happy memories. Harder ones might include discovering that you are codependent, learning to stand up for yourself, or becoming more financially aware as you separate finances. ***Remember, you can find gratitude in everything!***

EXERCISE 20—God's Eyes

In this exercise, I ask you to imagine your higher power as though they are standing with you or surrounding you— witnessing your thoughts, words, and actions. Now imagine your ex is standing in front of you and imagine seeing them through God's eyes (whatever "God" may be for you). This may be difficult, especially if visualizing is hard for you. But recall the infinite forgiveness, compassion, hope, and love God has for us all (and try to imagine your ex from this place). If you find this too difficult, you can think of the love an idealized mother or father would have for their child. Let this idea of unconditional love guide how you see your ex.

EXERCISE 21—Daily Affirmations

Our thoughts and self-talk are incredibly powerful. Sometimes, we are moving through our days using negative affirmations, saying things like, "I'm so stupid," or "I'm never going to get this right." When we do this, we are limiting our reality and creating a low energetic vibration that does not serve us in any way and leaves us feeling depleted. Finding positive affirmations is relatively easy and sets your mood and mindset for the day (or night).

You can find ideas for your personal affirmations on the internet or in the many books that exist on the topic. One of my favorite authors is Louise Hay—she also has several online resources, including free recordings you can listen to in the background during your morning or evening routines. The key to your positive affirmation is that you will say it as if it is already true...whether or not you believe it. By stating it as if it is already true, you are creating the space for it to be true, through visualizing it and experiencing it, which will support your best possible outcome.

For this exercise, you are asked to engage in this behavior as much as possible, but at the very least in the morning or at night. It doesn't take much time and since you're already talking to yourself all day, anyway, you may as well use mindful awareness to attend to what you're saying and turn it into a positive affirmation. It is a good idea to repeat positive affirmations several times over—at least three times. An example of this is, "My divorce is working out in the best possible way for all parties." You can use this any time you notice anxiety or discomfort arising during your divorce process.

Suggested Reading Resources

Boundaries and Codependency

The Language of Letting Go: Daily Meditations for Codependents, by Melody Beattie

Codependent No More: How to Stop Controlling Others and Start Caring for Yourself, by Melody Beattie

Codependent No More Workbook, by Melody Beattie

Boundaries by Henry Cloud and John Townsend

"NO" Is a Complete Sentence: Learning the Sacredness of Personal Boundaries, by Megan LeBoutillier

Facing Codependence: What It Is, Where It Comes From, Who It Sabotages in Our Lives, by Pia Mellody

Awakening in Time by Jacquelyn Small

Co-Parenting

Cooperative Parenting and Divorce: Shielding Your Child from Conflict, by Susan Blythe Boyan and Ann Marie Termini

The Coparents' Communication Handbook: Answers to Your Top Twenty Questions, by Susan Blythe Boyan and Ann Marie Termini

Forgiveness

The Art of Forgiveness, Lovingkindness, and Peace, by Jack Kornfield

Forgiving and Reconciling: Bridges to Wholeness and Hope, by Everett L. Worthington Jr.

Spiritual and Self-Development

A Course In Miracles (Combined Volume), scribed by Helen Schucman

The Miracle of Living Without Anger, by Bradley P. Barris

The Gifts of Imperfection: Let Go of Who You Think You're Supposed to Be and Embrace Who You Are, by Brené Brown

How to Meditate: A Practical Guide to Making Friends With Your Mind, by Pema Chodrôn

When Things Fall Apart: Heart Advice for Difficult Times, by Pema Chodrôn

Trust Life: Love Yourself Every Day with Wisdom from Louise Hay, by Louise Hay

You Can Heal Your Life, by Louise Hay

Healing After Loss: Daily Meditations for Working through Grief, by Martha W. Hickman

Feel the Fear and Do It Anyway: Dynamic Techniques for Turning Fear, Indecision and Anger Into Power, Action and Love, by Susan Jeffers.

The Dance of Anger: A Woman's Guide to Changing the Patterns of Intimate Relationships, by Harriet Lerner

Relationship: Are You Sure You Want One, by Simone Milasas and Brendon West

The Cow in the Parking Lot: A Zen Approach to Overcoming Anger, by Leonard Scheff and Susan Edmiston

The Power of the Spoken Word, by Florence Scovel Shinn

I Hear You: The Surprisingly Simple Skill Behind Extraordinary Relationships, by Michael S. Sorensen

The Mindful Woman: Gentle Practices for Restoring Calm, Finding Balance and Opening Your Heart, by Sue Patton Thoele

A Return to Love: Reflections on the Principles of A Course in Miracles, by Marianne Williamson

Books for Children

(The following books were suggested by Dr. Carbery to assist children with the divorce process)

Dinosaurs Divorce: A Guide for Changing Families, by Laurie Kransy Brown and Marc Brown

I Don't Want to Talk about It, by Jeanie Franz Ransom

Jessica's Two Families: Helping Children Learn to Cope with Blended Households, by Lynne Hugo, LPCC

Do You Sing Twinkle: A Story About Remarriage and New Family, by Sandra Levins

Was It the Chocolate Pudding: A Story for Little Kids about Divorce, by Sandra Levins

Two Homes, by Claire Masurel

When My Parents Forgot How to Be Friends, by Jennifer Moore-Mallinos

Standing On My Own Two Feet: A Child's Affirmation of Love in the Midst of Divorce, by Tamara Schmitz

Book References

Beattie, M. (1990). *The Language of Letting Go.* Center City, Minnesota: Hazelden.

Boyan, S.B. and Termini, A. (2003). *Cooperative Parenting and Divorce: Shielding Your Child From Conflict.* Atlanta, Georgia: Active Parenting Publishers.

Brown, C. B. (2012). *Daring Greatly: How the Courage to Be Vulnerable Transforms the Way We Live, Love, Parent, and Lead.* New York, New York: Gotham.

Carlsmith K.M., Wilson T.D., Gilbert D.T. (2008). "The Paradoxical Consequences of Revenge." *Journal of Personality and Social Psychology.* 95, 1316-24. PMID 10925285 DOI: 10.1037/a0012165

Chapman, G. (1992). *The Five Love Languages: How to Express Heartfelt Commitment to Your Mate.* Chicago, Illinois: Northfield Publishing.

Chapman, G. (2006). *The Five Languages of Apology.* Chicago, Illinois: Northfield Publishing.

De Quervain, D., Fischbacher, U., Treyer, V., Schellhammer, M., Schnyder, U., Buck, A. & Fehr, E. (2004). "The Neural Science of Altruistic Punishment." *Science* 305. 1245–58.

Elkins, D. (1998). *Beyond Religion*. Wheaton, Indiana: Quest Books.

Kelly, A.C., Zuroff, D.C., & Shapira, L.B. (2009). "Soothing Oneself and Resisting Self-Attacks: The Treatment of Two Intrapersonal Deficits in Depression Vulnerability." *Cognitive Therapy and Research*, 33, 301–313.

Kondō, M., & Hirano, C. (2014). *The Life-Changing Magic of Tidying Up: The Japanese Art of Decluttering and Organizing* (First American edition.). Berkeley, CA: Ten Speed Press.

Kübler-Ross, E. (1997). *The Wheel of Life*. New York, New York: Touchstone.

May, R. (2007). *Love and Will*. New York, New York: W.W. Norton & Company, Inc.

McCullough, M.E., Kurzban, R., Tabak, B.A. (2010). "Evolved Mechanisms for Revenge and Forgiveness." In M. Mikulincer and P. R. Shaver (2010) *Human aggression and violence: Causes, manifestations, and consequences*, 221-239. Washington, DC: American Psychologist Association.

Raffel, L. (1997). *Should I Stay or Should I Go: A Guide to Controlled Separation*. Chicago, Illinois: Contemporary Books.

Taylor, J. (2008). *A Stroke of Insight*. New York, New York: Penguin Random House, LLC.

Williamson, M. (1992). *A Return to Love: Reflections on the Principles of "A Course in Miracles."* New York, New York: HarperCollins Publishers, Inc.

Worthington, Jr., E.(2003). *Forgiving and Reconciling: Bridges to Wholeness and Hope*. Downers Grove, Illinois: Intervarsity Press.

Yarnell, L.M. & Neff, K.D. (2013) "Self-Compassion, Interpersonal Conflict Resolutions, and Well-being." *Self and Identity*, 12:2, 146-159, DOI: 10.1080/15298868.2011.649545

About the Author

Dr. Rebecca Harvey is a mind/body, neurobiologically-focused psychologist who specializes in providing a highly personalized therapy experience for her private practice clients. Her work is aimed at improving life satisfaction by reducing the stress and drama caused by emotional reactivity. She assists many clients who are contemplating, moving through, or healing from divorce. This is done by helping clients connect with their deeper goal of happiness and well-being and keeping this goal at the forefront during the divorce process. She touts cultivation of mindfulness, or mind-body presence, as well as compassion and forgiveness as significant factors in maintaining a commitment to a loving divorce process.

Dr. Harvey's interest in the power of the mind-body connection began in California in 1998 when she began practicing yoga while earning her undergraduate degree in psychology at California State University, Northridge. Beginning her studies in mind-body work in 2000 at the National Holistic Institute in California, she trained as a massage therapist gaining deeper insight into the impact of emotional trauma on the body and the interplay of somatic illness and mental health. She earned her master's and doctoral degrees from Pepperdine University focusing on the intersection of psychotherapy, trauma, mind-body connection, and the neurobiology of the therapy process. In August of 2013, she completed a 200-hour yoga teacher training at Dallas Yoga Center, deepening her knowledge of mind-body connection. In addition to her Dallas-based and online psychotherapy practice and corporate speaking engagements, she runs workshops for individuals interested in beginning or deepening mindfulness meditation practice. You can connect with Dr. Harvey on social media, Instagram, Twitter, and Facebook @DrRebeccaHarvey, or through her website: DrRebeccaHarvey.com.

REBECCA HARVEY, PSY. D.